Praise for

YOU DESERVE
THE TRUTH

"In this beautifully written, smart, and soulful book, Erica Williams Simon gives us what we all need more of: The knowing that life, at its best, is more about wonder than certainty. With *You Deserve the Truth*, Erica invites us beyond the old stories we've been told about ourselves and into the wonder of our dreams, hopes, and love—so we can find our truth and purpose there."

—Glennon Doyle, author of the #1 *New York Times* bestseller *Love Warrior* and founder of Together Rising

"[A] gratifying debut. . . . Millennials looking for advice from a perceptive peer will appreciate Simon's refreshingly blunt take on happiness."

—*Publishers Weekly*

"Erica is the girlfriend everyone deserves: full of wisdom, grace, and unwavering honesty. *You Deserve the Truth* is the smart and all too real guidebook for anyone striving to craft an authentic and inspired life from the ground up. Erica's willingness to share the messy parts of her truth is a needed reminder for the rest of us to live ours."

—Franchesca Ramsey, author of *Well, That Escalated Quickly* and host of MTV's *Decoded*

"Our lives are filled with story; Simon's book deconstructs her personal stories about fear, dreams, work, money, time, faith, and love . . . Simon mixes her personal experience with national and global examples of nascent narrative intelligence. Her writing style is readable and engaging, and her message matters."

—*Booklist*

"For a straightforward and honest look under the hood of the human experience, soiled but also blessed by what social media has done to it, Erica Williams Simon's *You Deserve the Truth* will act as a road map that can feel like an iron fist in a cashmere glove: delicate and warm but unflinching and equable at once. If we are, as she says, all wayfinders, Erica is the closest thing we get to a guide."

—Leandra Medine, founder of Man Repeller

YOU DESERVE
THE TRUTH

Change the Stories that Shaped Your World
and Build a World-Changing Life

Erica Williams Simon

GALLERY BOOKS

New York   London   Toronto   Sydney   New Delhi

Gallery Books
An Imprint of Simon & Schuster, Inc.
1230 Avenue of the Americas
New York, NY 10020

First Gallery Books trade paperback edition January 2020

GALLERY BOOKS and colophon are registered trademarks of Simon & Schuster, Inc.

For information about special discounts for bulk purchases, please contact Simon & Schuster Special Sales at 1-866-506-1949 or business@simonandschuster.com.

The Simon & Schuster Speakers Bureau can bring authors to your live event. For more information or to book an event, contact the Simon & Schuster Speakers Bureau at 1-866-248-3049 or visit our website at www.simonspeakers.com.

Manufactured in the United States of America

10 9 8 7 6 5 4 3 2 1

Library of Congress Cataloging-in-Publication Data

Names: Simon, Erica Williams, author.
Title: You deserve the truth : change the stories that shaped your world and build a world-changing life / Erica Williams Simon.
Description: New York : Gallery Books, [2019]
Identifiers: LCCN 2018028331| ISBN 9781501163258 (hardcover) | ISBN 9781501163272 (trade paper) | ISBN 9781501163265 (ebook)
Subjects: LCSH: Conduct of life. | Self-realization. | Success.
Classification: LCC BJ1589 .S495 2019 | DDC 170/.44—dc23
LC record available at https://lccn.loc.gov/2018028331

ISBN 978-1-5011-6325-8
ISBN 978-1-5011-6327-2 (pbk)
ISBN 978-1-5011-6326-5 (ebook)

To the One who creates something out of nothing.

I dedicate these words and everything that I am to You.

CONTENTS

INTRODUCTION

It was a cold Sunday morning in January, barely thirty degrees outside of our church. Snow was expected to hit the Washington, DC, area soon, and although none was falling yet, the air outside was bitter. I was inside, standing in the front of the sanctuary singing with the worship team, like I did every Sunday. At sixteen years old, I was the only teenager in the adult group. And no, it wasn't just because my father was the pastor. It was because this church, this ministry, this gift of music and worship and service was my life. From the time that my parents founded our church in our home when I was nine months old, there was no place that felt more like home to me. On this day, thanks to my thick tights and enough rocking, clapping, and arm-waving to rival a low-impact aerobics class, I had worked up a light sweat. I loved singing in church. I'd have rather been right there, holding a microphone and singing songs to God with the people I loved, than anywhere else in the world. I felt free. I felt alive.

If you've never experienced worship in a black church, the only way I can possibly describe what it feels like is to call it a high. It takes you away from where you are and floats you somewhere in the clouds. Suddenly you are before the Throne of God. Or in the Holy of Holies. Or on holy ground. Or whatever euphemism you choose to describe the overwhelming presence of the Divine. You are miles away from your worldly troubles and concerns, pouring out everything that is inside of you. And somehow you feel as if the most intimate parts of yourself are being received as the most precious gift.

I'm explaining all of this because on that day, the worship was pretty intense. The Spirit was "having his way," which is what we say whenever we disregard the schedule and just go with the flow. And me? I was "higher" than usual. We all were. And so was Daddy. He had walked up in front of the pulpit, singing along with us. He was wearing his forest-green suit, standing six-foot-three, a small glittering gold cross around his neck. Without any effort, he and I suddenly found ourselves engaged in a musical call-and-response, back-and-forth. I wish I could remember what we were singing. All I know is that I was following his lead—he would sing something and I would repeat—and that it sounded beautiful.

As the shouts and tears quieted down and the music slowed, we went back to our seats and Daddy began to preach. He instructed us to open to Matthew Chapter 9 and began to read the story of the new wine. In it, Jesus compares the new life that the gospel offers everyone to new wine. Daddy started to expound on the opportunity of an abundant, new life being available to all who seek it. He was on fire that morning, walking back and forth, out from behind the pulpit, close to us in the congregation. As the church was erupting with amens and claps, he walked back behind the pulpit and paused like he did when he was about to say something good. "New life!" he said, as we hung on to his every word. "New li—"

Before he could finish saying it a second time, he slumped. He leaned and grabbed the side of the pulpit to catch himself, but within seconds, he fell to the ground. When I see the scene in my mind, this is when the ground shakes. I feel a physical tremble, like what you imagine would happen if the tallest, oldest, widest tree in the forest suddenly tipped over, the thud shaking the firmament for miles around. I am certain that didn't happen, but I also wonder: How could anything in the world not have felt the impact of this, an actual earthquake?

The moments after are a blur. Daddy on the ground. Me running, almost reflexively, to the bathroom and slamming the door, trying to shut out the scary scene taking place around me. Yells to call 911. Me doubled over the sink, dry heaving, crying, "*It's not okay. It's not okay. Please let it be okay.*" Then the stretcher rushing past me, my mother running beside it. Me in the front seat of my aunt's car as she drove me and my nine-year-old, cherub-faced sister home to wait for news.

Hours later, I remember opening the front door when I saw my mother and my father's best friend, his co-pastor, pull into the driveway. Her face shattered when she saw me, like a piece of glass hit with a bullet. I don't remember her saying the words "Daddy died." But I do remember running.

When we all went back to the hospital that evening to do whatever it is that people do when their people die, they told me that I could go into a room to be with him for a moment. I walked in to where he was lying and held his hand, now cool, his gold wedding band cutting tightly into his finger. I placed my head on his chest, and cried and cried. I cried to try to stop the ache inside of me, but it only got stronger. Silent tears fell, my throat and eyes burning. I said, "I love you, Daddy" over and over again, until the words lost meaning and I wasn't sure if I was actually still saying them or not.

I knew that others were waiting to come into the room and have their moment, so I gathered myself, kissed him on the cheek, and for no particular reason other than that the refrain was fresh in my head and I had no other words, I whispered, "New life."

And that was that. Those were the last words my daddy said. And they were the last words I said to him. *New life.*

Those words and that story would guide much of the next decade of my life. Life A.D. After Daddy. My faith, my personality, even my politics, were all grounded in a belief that new life was possible. That a better life should be accessible to anyone. That rebirth, re-creation, a hard reset was our birthright. I felt a pull toward anything that could create a new reality for me, for the people I loved, and for people who needed and deserved more. I have tried with all of my might to bend those words to breaking—to mean more than the makeovers presented on reality television or the come-ups that we see on Instagram. I believe that it is something more. "New life" is why, after college, I chose a career that focused on helping people transform their communities and the country through activism and advocacy. I believe that everyone deserves to have a life free from the shackles of oppression and the systems of injustice and inequality that have held them captive.

And I guess in some ways, that story and its meaning are what led to this book. The words were ringing in my ears as I walked away, at twenty-seven, from an outwardly successful but secretly unhappy life on a professional hamster wheel. I didn't know what I was walking toward, nor was I fully clear on how I'd ended up in the life I was walking away from, but I was determined to discover what was holding me back from the life I craved—one free from anxiety and fear, from comparison and discontent, from instability and insecurity, from endless longing and lack, from confusion and disappointment.

Now, having gone on that journey and essentially succeeded, I am committed to spreading this gospel, this good news: Life can be better than *this*. You do not have to be held captive to the current reality you are living, the one created by old stories, myths, and systems designed to suffocate you and make you conform.

You do not have to live a life breathlessly chasing success, fighting the demons of self-doubt, and engaged in constant warfare with your circumstances. No matter your financial background, age, gender, or race; no matter how much you have screwed up in the past, or how confused you are, or how much you feel like a fraud. It doesn't matter that you have absolutely no idea what in the world you are doing, or how much Instagram and Facebook make you feel like you should. Even if the day's news makes you feel like the whole world is spiraling out of control, you can have a new life, better than the one that all the statistics promised you.

But change involves much more than a motivational mantra.

Hear me out, let it sink in: You really can have peace, clarity of purpose, direction, and success in this hectic, broken world. And you can have a hand in fixing that hectic, broken world at the same time.

You may be thinking: *Sure. Sí se puede. But how?*

Well, unbeknownst to me, when I first embarked on this journey, the answer to that very question was hidden in the second half of my father's sermon, the part he never got to preach. The scripture in Matthew 9:17 talks about how the only way to carry and hold on to that new wine (or new life), is to discard the old wineskins, the stretched leather bottles that held the old wine. If you try to pour the new wine in the old weathered skins, they will burst and break. We must pour it into something entirely new. In other words, we can't change our current lives and realities—our hopes, dreams, finances, or even our communities—without first changing the framework, the container, that holds them.

That container is made of stories. The stretched, weathered, and worn stories that we have been taught, that we have consumed, that have built our worlds, shaped everything around us, carried us from birth to now. Those stories shaped what we believed was possible.

To continuously pour our vision for a new life and new world into a space already shaped and stretched by the beliefs and untrue stories of the broken world that fueled your discontent in the first place is a waste of time. And in order to build a new life and a new world, one that lasts beyond the short-term encouragement of an inspirational quote or the short-lived excitement of a new job, we must recognize and change the stories that we believe. Everyone who has come and gone before us—those who lived a life constrained and unfulfilled *and* those who were brave enough to break out—would want us to know the truth. And this is what I am sharing with you now. In some ways, I am, as the poet Rupi Kaur says, "the product of my ancestors getting together and deciding these stories need to be told." And these new stories that we create together must be built not on fantasies and myths, but on truth. Each and every one of us deserves it.

The story of my awakening led to the book you are holding in your hands today. Maybe you are feeling—or have felt before—the same way that I felt when I decided that I wanted a new life.

Every day I talk to overwhelmed and unfulfilled people like you— many in their twenties and thirties—who have that nagging feeling in the pit of their stomach. Fighting to be optimistic and hopeful and yet terrified that nothing around them—not data, not the news, not the lives of the people they hold dear—justifies their hope that they can have a successful life of radical happiness, purpose, and impact.

I do not purport to have all of the answers. But here is what I do believe: The freedom—personal and collective—that we are so desperately seeking can only appear and be sustained if we are willing to create new stories to hold us. Here's mine.

PART I

CHAPTER 1

THE MIC DROP

pounded away at the keys like a bass drum, as if I was telling off the laptop itself and not just the man on the receiving end of the note I was crafting.

> Dear [name redacted],
>   Today is my last day. It has been a pleasure working with
>   you. I wish you the best.
>   Erica

Send.

And that was it. Just like that I quit my job. No warning, no notice. One angry email and suddenly I was free. (And unemployed.)

I logged out of my work email for the last time, shut my laptop, and calmly walked down the soft carpeted stairs in our new loft apartment, heart pumping, feeling exhilarated, light-headed, and somewhat bewildered at the same time.

"I quit!" I said, to no one in particular, although my husband of two weeks and BFF since I was seventeen years old (hereafter known as Lifetime Bae or LB), was sitting right there.

The words sounded to my ears as if they were coming out of someone else's mouth.

"Wait, what?" he said, looking at me as if I must have been joking. He knew that I had spent the last thirty minutes fuming about how an incompetent colleague had somehow messed up my paycheck, and that I was in the throes of trying to sort it out before returning to work on what was supposed to be my first day back after our honeymoon. He knew that I was sick of this job, that I hated my boss, that it was demoralizing to have to argue about getting paid after having also been told via email that, in my absence, my role had been changed and that upon my return I would be doing something that I was entirely overqualified for. He knew that for months I had been questioning my entire career trajectory, wondering what was next and feeling bothered by the minimal amount of impact I was having in a profession that was supposedly all about changing the world. He knew all of that because I spent every waking moment telling him. But quitting? That was not in the plans.

I could tell this story now in a way that makes you think that I am a fierce, fearless queen for dropping the mic and exiting stage left. But the truth is that my mic drop didn't feel fierce and powerful. It felt more like *I can't hold this anymore, I can't hold this anymore, I CAN'T HOLD THIS ANYMO— Oh my God, the mic is on the floor.*

The entire experience was like finally killing a fly that has been buzzing around your head and terrorizing you all day, but then realizing that in the process of swatting you have knocked over everything on your desk and are now surrounded by a mess of papers, a broken picture frame, and a spilled cup of coffee dripping down your keyboard. In other words, I really hadn't meant to swing that hard.

"I quit," I calmly repeated. Except this time, I said the words so slowly that I began to question whether or not I was having a stroke. "I quit my job."

What had I just done?

Sure, that job had been demoralizing for a whole host of reasons—not the least of which was a dishonest, manipulative boss who lacked integrity and the fact that I was paraded around to donors as their prized black girl (the only one in an organization whose mission was to fight for equal rights for minorities). But the truth is that for a nonprofit, it actually paid pretty well. Certainly more than I'd made at any other nonprofit job previously. And if that alone wasn't a reason to stay, I had just gotten married. We had just moved into a new apartment and splurged on new "we're real grown-ups now" furniture that was being delivered in a few days. There were bills to pay, things to do, and a life to build.

Almost immediately the following thoughts ran through my head:

I am not a job quitter.

You don't quit jobs.

Girl, what? You just quit your job?

Over email? Who raised you?

We don't just quit.

No, no, no, sis.

You have watched Jerry Maguire *one too many times, but you are not Tom Cruise.*

You are a young black woman with a nonprofit salary and student loans.

Correction: You were *a young black woman with a nonprofit salary and student loans.*

Now you just have loans.

Chile.

Chile, chile, chile.

In case it isn't clear, I was not the type of person to quit a job with no plan, no next move, no salary and benefits waiting on the other side. I was not a person with the Suze Orman–recommended six months of savings in the bank or a Rolodex of wealthy relatives or friends of the family who could bankroll a "sabbatical." (If you're anything like me, you've read a dozen stories where the character swears up and down that they are not the type of person to do something crazy like quit a job with no Plan B—and then a mere two pages later you read some casually mentioned detail like a rich husband, a trust fund, cashed-out stock options, a lawsuit settlement, or a lottery ticket that makes them *exactly* the type of person you and I would think does something like quit a job with no Plan B. I assure you, that will not happen here.)

So why had I done it? Were things really that bad? What did I really have to complain about?

I had a career that, on paper, anyone would have been proud of. It had many of the marks of Meaningful Millennial Success. At twenty-seven, I was on a bunch of "30 under 30" lists as a rising political star, a policy advocate, and a commentator on CNN, HBO, and MTV. I had been written about by the *Washington Post* and *Politico*, published in the *Harvard Business Review* and *Time* magazine, and had won countless awards for the work I'd done to engage young people in social change. I was an Aspen Institute Ideas Fellow. A World Economic Forum Global Shaper. An NAACP One to Watch. I'd even been to Davos (must be pronounced Daaaah-vos with a deep, breathy "Daaaah"). When Swizz Beatz asks, "*Oh you fancy huh?*" my bio would indicate that he was talking directly to me. And I was grateful.

But we all know that a bio is essentially nothing more than a polished highlight reel. It doesn't ever tell the full story. And mine, behind the scenes, looked very different from the one the *Essence* magazine profile about me would have you believe. The truth is I was miserable.

I was cash-poor, chronically underpaid, routinely reprimanded for speaking or writing messages of empowerment and truth outside of the confines of my organization, and regularly exposed to harassment, sexism, and racism, all while working hard to convince others to join me in the fight to change the world. Despite outwardly professing a belief that I could do anything and an intellectual understanding that I was a part of one of the most privileged, technologically advanced generations in history, deep down inside I was crippled by the gap between what I heard/thought/understood was expected of me and what I actually felt capable of doing. And, what exactly was expected of me by my elders, colleagues, society, and even my peers was, frankly, quite confusing.

These are just a few of the shoulds that floated through my mind on any given day:

- Work your way up the ladder; be committed and patient.

- But also be an innovative entrepreneur that seizes every opportunity to build something new.

- Don't care about money because you're a selfless change agent.

- But also somehow make enough money to pay off your student loans, take care of your parents in their old age, and purchase a beautiful house.

- Be cerebral, intellectual, and professional so that you can be taken seriously.

- But also be wildly creative, free-spirited, and youthful so that you bring the millennial edge that everyone wants from you.

- Be balanced, spiritually grounded, and whole.

- But also don't talk about any religion or spiritual practice. (Unless it's yoga. Yoga is cool. God is not.)

- Don't be vain or selfie-obsessed.

- But still post enough selfies a day to look confident and grow your social media following so that you can have lots of followers and bring attention to the things that matter more than the selfies.

- Be present and always in the moment.

- But also be online all the time, ever reachable, and in touch with what is happening everywhere else.

- Be proud of your identity. Talk about it, represent it well. Black girl magic FTW.

- But also don't identify with labels or talk too much about your race or gender, so as not to alienate others.

- Your biological clock is ticking, so start a family.

- But not now because you should probably have a house first, right?

- But don't buy a house because the market is shot and it's no longer a good investment.

- So now that you have a man, go ahead and have a baby. But not before you establish your career.

- Know your place and follow the rules. Respect your elders.

- But don't forget to break all the rules and be "iconic."

- Say you want to change the world.

- But don't get too specific about how or what that actually means because no one wants to hear about your politics all the time.

- And whatever you do, *get money.*

- But don't think about, desire or talk about it. Just get it. (And then say it isn't important.)

The truth is, I wasn't just tired of my job. I was tired of it all.

I spent the rest of the day, after my abrupt finale email, dipping in and out of sleep, trying to breathe, and hoping that I would wake up and the day would start over. Here I was, taking the first step to find my purpose, live my truth, and win at making the world better on my terms, come hell or high water. And that step was to jump off the merry-go-round, even while it was still spinning.

Patron Saint Oprah says that sometimes, after God has whispered something quietly in your ear enough times and you still haven't responded, He will hit you upside the head to get your attention. And I was now paying attention.

But long before I quit my job, my soul knew that this path I was on—as standard as it may have appeared—was not going to lead me to the life that I deserved. And it didn't feel like it was truly going to change the world either, which is what I wanted to do most of all. So if quitting my job was the push that I needed to walk away from it all and figure out where I'd gone wrong—and how to get right—so be it.

The day I made the choice to walk away from my job, I was actually choosing to walk away from my life—the identity, expectations, and path that had felt both familiar and unsustainable. I wanted more, I wanted *better.* Better than all of this. But admitting that was terrifying. I felt ungrateful. And worse, I felt as if in quitting, I was admitting that I somehow couldn't handle living the kind of life that everyone else seemed to be managing just fine.

That night, I walked into the bathroom, looked in the mirror, and asked the woman staring back at me, "What is wrong with you?" I said it over and over again, until the tears fell like rain. I wasn't just asking, "What is wrong with you that you would abruptly quit a good-paying, stable, relatively easy job with no plan?" I was really asking, "What is wrong with you, that you are not content? That you have no direction? That you are unsatisfied, unfulfilled, and unsure? That despite how it may look on the outside, you are wholly unable to master this life that you have cobbled together. What, really, is wrong with you?"

That question remained on a constant loop in my head for weeks. I heard it every time I lied and told someone that I'd quit my job to start a consulting firm. I heard it every time I pretended to know exactly what I was doing and that I had a plan. Every time that people told me how proud they were that I had "walked away from the rat race" and how jealous they were that I was "my own boss," I heard the question. I heard it every one of the ten times a day I updated my website, writing and rewriting my bio to sound more confident about my past and future than I really was. Not a day went by that I didn't follow up "the question" with another: "Are you a fraud?" "Are you weak?" "Are you lazy?" "Are you entitled?" "Are you delusional?"

But I wasn't a fraud or weak or lazy or entitled or delusional. And you aren't either.

THE CROOKED ROOM THEORY

One day, I was flipping through unread books on my bookshelf, looking for a read that would take my mind off my existential crisis.

I decided to pick up *Sister Citizen* by Melissa Harris-Perry, a book about the political identity of black women in America. I hoped that I would drift off into the reliably nerdy and unemotional world of political theory and, for just a moment, forget about my personal sorrow. Instead, to my surprise, I found staring back at me, hidden in the pages of this sociopolitical critique, the explanation for my current crippling self-doubt and perpetual quandary.

In the book, Harris-Perry describes a sociological concept called the Crooked Room Theory. It's an idea based on a post–World War II psychology study about field dependence: how people locate the upright position within a defined space. In one part of the study, subjects were seated in a crooked chair in a crooked room, and then asked to align themselves perpendicularly with the ceiling (aka straight). As you can imagine, it wasn't an easy task. Most perceived themselves as straight only in relation to their surroundings. They could actually be tilted by as much as *thirty-five degrees* but still report that they felt perfectly straight, simply because they were aligned with images and objects around them that were equally tilted. Some managed to get themselves more or less upright regardless of how crooked the surrounding images were, a feat not only difficult but, I would imagine, pretty disorienting. Imagine believing, *knowing* that you are straight, and seeing everything around you—the floor, the seating, the walls, the paintings—all crooked? Harris-Perry explains, "It can be so hard to stand up straight and orient yourself when your surroundings are tilted by your own perceptions and those of others."

As I read that sentence, my eyes welled up with tears (yes, I was crying a lot in those days), and I highlighted her words so hard that the yellow bled through the pages beneath it.

This theory perfectly explained my current situation.

I had spent years trying to find and be myself—my vibrant, inspired, ambitious, values-driven self—in a professional space where no one looked like me or saw the world the way I did; where the expectations of how I should think, move, and grow were ever-present but unnatural. I had tried and tried—job after job, project after project—to contort myself and find happiness in doing what I was *supposed* to do, what I saw other people doing . . . to be like what I saw hanging on the walls around me. And it simply hadn't worked.

For years, I'd leaned and bent to conform to the volatile, conflicting, and ever-evolving expectations of the world around me.

So when I quit my job and walked away, I was finally trying to stand up straight. And sure enough, I felt crazy.

But I wasn't crazy. And this was not my fault. The room—my entire world—was crooked. Every image that I saw, every story that I had been told, every dream that I had dreamt, was shaped by values that caused me to contort and twist and look sideways at the world.

Right there, in my living room, I resolved never to ask what was wrong with me again. And I want you, right now, to do the same.

———

As I look around, it seems like many of us today—especially those of us in our twenties and thirties—are trying to stand up straight and find our bearings while everything around us feels and is somehow *off*. And the way I look at it, when you're standing in a crooked room, you have two options: You either stand up straight and feel crazy, or you bend.

We've been doing one or both for most of our lives.

I don't know your specific story. You may have had a successful career thus far, or it may have been a string of disappointments and false starts. You may have graduated from a top-tier school, or you may still be plugging away, part-time, through community college while working a nine-to-five. You may come from a "perfect" family, or you may have a family so dysfunctional that it makes Honey Boo Boo's parents look like the Obamas. The truth is, your story could differ from mine in any number of ways. But I wouldn't waste my time sharing it if I wasn't willing to bet that you *have*, at some point, felt exactly as I felt the day I up and quit.

Odds are good that somewhere deep down inside, you've felt the same mix of frustration, confusion, aimlessness, self-doubt, righteous anger, shame, and anxiety at how different the world is from your expectations, and how your own life is panning out in it.

How do I know this? Because the statistics say so. No generation has been more studied, analyzed, and opined about than ours. The resulting data paints a striking portrait of our collective discontent. Economic insecurity, global instability, rapid technological advancement, and the breakdown of critical social institutions like public education, government, and religion have created the perfect cocktail for generational crisis. (Those factors also point to the inevitable decline of empire and the grave state of the American Experiment, but I digress. I'll leave my politics out of it . . . for now.)

Despite us achieving higher rates of an increasingly higher-cost education in an unforgiving job market that now demands more of it, the value and quality of the education itself has declined dramatically in the past fifty years. And none of it has translated into increased employment prospects.

Many people in their twenties and thirties today are chronically unemployed and underemployed: 44 percent of recent college graduates who *are* working are working in low-wage jobs that do not even require a college degree. Want to know why so many of us have made-up job titles that our parents scoff at? Because a lack of upward professional mobility has forced us to be creative and design positions, work, and titles that have never existed before.

Stagnant wages and the exorbitant cost of college mean that those who have entered the workforce are drowning in student debt, spending most of our paychecks on sky-high rents, replacing the homeownership debt many of our parents had at our age with credit card debt, and with nothing but small purchases to show for it.

A whopping 51 percent of eighteen to twenty-nine-year-olds surveyed by the Harvard Institute of Politics were more fearful than hopeful about the future. I would imagine that at least some of the other 49 percent were hopeful in that "I am choosing to ignore the signs and stay positive" kind of way. (And note that the poll was taken pre-election 2016. I would assume that the near daily reminders of Armageddon brought to you by the Trump White House have changed the hopeful to hopeless ratio just a bit.)

And yet poll after poll also says that despite our economic and social realities, millennials are an optimistic bunch. It's like we're gritting our teeth in fear and yet forcing ourselves to smile anyway. Which is quite wonderful. To a point. But that determined optimism in the face of daunting circumstances also goes hand in hand with high rates of anxiety, depression, suicide, and stress-related health problems.

These concerns go far beyond the traditional emotional markers of entering into adulthood. Authors Alexandra Robbins and Abby Wilner coined the term "quarterlife crisis" for the rite-of-passage, coming-of-age, stage-of-life drama that surrounds the transition into independence. Questions like "What if I'm afraid to grow up?" or "Could I be managing my money better?" are pretty standard for anyone, in any generation, when entering a new phase of responsibility.

But answering basic, coming-of-age life questions like those becomes far more complicated in our world today: We live in a society without safety nets, within a dystopian political climate in which every social issue—from institutional racism and police brutality, to corporate greed and crashing markets, to campus sexual assault and reproductive rights, to global terrorism, Islamophobia, and hate crimes—is fighting for front-page attention. In a landscape where societal norms and expectations are redefined at a faster-than-lightning pace and then shoved in front of us on our phones all day long, figuring out who you are, where you want to be, and how you want to navigate life is harder than it's ever been.

Technology hasn't helped, either. What many thought was going to be the silver bullet to provide everything that our generation would need to thrive and compete in the new world has also brought with it a host of challenges that make perception, progress, and identifying reality harder than they have ever been. While technology has allowed us to meet people and see things we would never otherwise have seen, it also makes us assume that everything is easy, or right within reach. In that way, the internet acts as kind of a side-view mirror, except *objects in mirror may be farther, not closer, than they appear.* We may have far more to look at and be inspired by than ever before (including the airbrushed lives of our peers), but the false sense of authenticity makes us believe that all of the opportunity that we see is at our fingertips, when in reality, thanks to the lack of supporting infrastructure in the off-line world, much of it is far beyond a normal arm's reach.

The headlines and magazine covers lay out a grave and dire assessment of our generation. And yet those same headlines are usually followed by an "inspirational" piece about a beautiful, successful millennial who seems to have it all. Somehow he or she is making it work and thriving in the midst of this chaos. And they are making it look so . . . easy. When we see those glittering success stories, packaged perfectly in a 250-word magazine profile or a 50-word Instagram post, the fear of inadequacy within us rears its ugly head and brings on the self-loathing: We believe that despite the data, us not achieving exactly what we want to achieve is evidence of our own personal failings. He did it! She did it! Why can't we? We stare facts in the face—facts that *should* be a clear sign that maybe something is wrong with the room itself—and choose to believe that we are uniquely unqualified to live an epic life and change the world.

When I worked at Upworthy, a digital media company on a mission to spread stories about issues that matter and make them just as viral as cat videos and cooking demos, we had one motto: *Stories stick. Facts fade.* In other words, people don't remember facts. They remember the stories. In this context, it means that the facts that give justification for some if not all of our frustration fade in the face of stories about a small minority of über-successful millenials.

In the years since I made my choice to walk away, I have talked to countless people in their twenties and thirties who, like me, had at one point or another felt a quickening in their body, a longing and an urge to break free. From a job, from a relationship, from a career, from an overall way of being that seemed futile and . . . less than. Their stories aren't often highlighted in the media. They don't necessarily win the awards. But they are human. And a very real reminder that you are not alone. I've changed their names, but here are some of their stories.

———

Alicia is a twenty-five-year-old El Salvadoran immigrant who was the first in her family to go to college. Her family is proud and expects "big things" from her. They also expect her to help out with a portion of the family expenses. Young girls in her community look up to her. But Alicia doesn't have a mentor or any direction for her next steps. She remembers being a freshman in college and seeing so many young adults getting on board the Obama train and doing good in the world. She couldn't wait to do that too, but despite having graduated with honors after working her way through school (doing her first two years at community college and finishing up at a state university), she is barely making enough to live on as a program associate at a local nonprofit, let alone contribute anything financially to her family.

Alicia wants to change the world but also needs to make some money. Should she start her own small business like her parents did and forgo her dream of making a difference? Should she go back to school to get another degree that would increase her value in the workplace? But how in the world would she afford that? Because she's the first in her family to experience this journey, there's no one in her close network of elders to give her advice, so she reaches for it wherever she can. Her Instagram page is a flood of inspirational quotes, and her feed is full of women telling her to be a "girl boss" and "be great." But she still isn't quite sure what to do next, and she stays up nights, worried and anxious, afraid that time is running out for her to become the woman her parents risked it all for her to be.

Or there's Mia. Mia is a twenty-seven-year-old African American woman. After graduating college, she was chosen for the Teach for America program and has continued to teach in the public school system. Because of the low salary (and the fact that she spends her own money on supplies for her classroom as well as food, winter coats, and other essentials for her students), she has decided to move in with her mother while teaching. She's become increasingly "woke" and finds it hard to reconcile her new political awakening with the confines of the education system. Every day, she sees children come into her classroom who are in need of much more than what they will be tested on at the end of the semester, and her heart aches that she doesn't have the freedom or the support to give it to them. The high school where she is teaching is being shut down due to insufficient funding. She can continue teaching in another school and experience more of the same—being frustrated, underpaid, and heartbroken about how little impact she actually seems to be making. Or she can give up, take her considerable skills, and go into corporate America. She wonders if she can be of more help to young people in the long run somehow as a financially stable adult than she can struggling in this economy. She's questioning what impact she wants to have on the world and how that relates to her own passions and prospects.

Joel is a twenty-nine-year-old recent grad school graduate drowning in debt, who can't find a job and is starting to regret his decision to stay out of the job market for so long. He is currently sharing an apartment with two roommates who spend the majority of their time playing Xbox. He has been looking for a job for four months and is finding the job market unforgiving. Meanwhile, his girlfriend of four years is anxious, wondering when he is going to propose so they can start their life together. He is angry that his life is where it is at the end of his twenties.

Derrick is a thirty-year-old man living in Baltimore who is on the fast track in his business marketing career. He has a great idea for an app, but he doesn't know what the next best steps are to get it to market. He could probably scrape together enough money to hire someone, but it would take using all of his savings, and he doesn't know if it's worth the risk. He has also recently joined his local Black Lives Matter chapter—because, as for most young men and women of color—the current wave of cultural "wokeness" is personal to him. He knows what it's like to be stopped by the police while driving around his neighborhood for no reason at all. Yet he wonders how his growing passion for activism will impact his professional brand. And will his vocal presence on social media deter investors from helping him with his idea?

Or Meagan, a thirty-four-year-old white woman with a fantastic job who is afraid to take the next step in her career because her biological clock is ticking and she believes that, more than anything, quite frankly, she needs to find a man. She is convinced that her job and her ambition are what's stopping her from "having it all," and she doesn't know what to do because she knows her lack of a partner is a stain on her otherwise spotless life. She dies a little on the inside every time someone brushes past her accomplishments to ask why she isn't married yet and whether or not she wants children. She has "leaned in" so much she's about to fall off the cliff and has come to realize that pursuing your dreams is cool until it pushes you too far outside of what other people expect of you. Still, she's afraid to admit how lonely she is because it doesn't fit the image of the empowered, self-reliant woman she portrays herself to be.

And for every one of these stories, there are more hiding beneath the surface that even I am not privy to. Stories of heartbreak, trauma, family discord, battles with identity, racism, sexism, homophobia, illness—all of the side effects of living a human life.

These are all smart, hardworking people who have tried really hard to do the right thing, to play the cards they were dealt, to follow the rules laid out for them by society, and to sew the pieces of their life into the shiny, happy story that they have been told is both desirable and possible. All of them have stood on the precipice of some next step of adulthood—education, employment, entrepreneurship, marriage, even children—and have been told that now, after finally reaching this peak, anything is possible; they are well on their way to the "American Dream." All they have to do is start the right nonprofit, or marry the right partner, or come up with the right business idea, or run the right campaign, or wear the right size, or invest in the right stock, or get the right job, and they will find peace and joy.

And time and time again, after the graduation balloons have deflated and the student loan bills start pouring in, after the shiny business cards are ordered for the new gig and the reality that they still need a side hustle in order to live comfortably slaps them in the face, after the hopeful work to change the world and then the depressing realization that the systems they thought were going to help them change it are just as broken as the ones they set out to change, many people find themselves confused, dejected, bored with the monotony of life, and perhaps most maddening of all, not knowing exactly what to do next.

Perhaps one of these stories will stick with you in those moments when you are tempted to think that you alone are the problem, that you're just not trying hard enough. Read these stories without the Photoshop and filters of a Twitter bio. Peek behind the illusion of perfection and invincibility that we all desperately hide behind. If these people were here right now, they would tell you to look at their lives as proof. You are not alone nor are you crazy. We're all in this together.

Many of us feel like hot messes at best, miserable failures at worst, because we attribute the gap between our real life and the one we think we should be living to our own shortcomings. If I were only more *fill in the blank*: disciplined, outgoing, popular, focused, strong, savvy, educated, beautiful, feminine or masculine, intelligent, fit, effective. Then I would have the things that "they" told me I would have.

What a horrible, shame-filled story to believe. And it's one that isn't often grounded in truth.

Don't rush to question your sanity, competence, or strength when you feel as if you don't belong in the life that you are currently living or when you realize that following all of the rules to the best of your ability didn't (and won't) help you win. Nor should you call yourself a quitter when you decide that you no longer want to play "the game"—the one that tells you to keep running on that hamster wheel toward your wildest dreams without ever questioning the wheel itself or where those dreams came from.

Promise me—and yourself—that you will not believe that you, your person, your very existence is wrong before investigating the wrongness of the room around you. Because in a world that is hell-bent on telling each and every one of us at every turn who we are supposed to be, what is expected of us, and what we must do in order to buy or reach peak happiness, despite its own brokenness and instability, *of course* it's hard to stand—let alone walk, let alone confidently go in the direction of our dreams.

Recognizing that your experience is shaped by the realities of the world around you is not making an excuse. It is common sense.

Now that you acknowledge that fact, the bigger, more important questions are: What can we do about this crooked room? And what will it take for us to break down the walls of belief, behavior, and expectation that lead to discontent? How can we uncover the truth and live the powerful life that we deserve?

CHAPTER 2

THE ANSWER IS STORY

"The world is not made of atoms. It is made of stories."
—MURIEL RUKEYSER

I have long devoured the wisdom of the greatest self-help gurus. I'm a sucker for a feel-good self-improvement book, the tough, tell-it-like-it-is language of a motivational speech, the insight of a perfectly crafted TED Talk. Surely one of them, I thought, would help me hack my life into one of success, fulfillment, and impact during this life reset that I was now embarking on. As I flipped through the books, blogs, and YouTube videos, a central theme kept rising to the surface. The culprit of my discontent, they all seemed to be saying, was "story."

Just Google the phrase "change your story, change your life," and you'll see countless blogs, books, and quotes that all equate your external circumstances with the story inside your head. If they are to be believed, all of my peers and I are simply telling ourselves the wrong stories! If we could just snap out of it and tell ourselves the right ones, we could find peace and fulfillment.

Really. It must be true! All of my favorite motivational teachers—and Instagram—said so.

Tony Robbins promised me that "a powerful story leads to a life of opportunity. The first step in changing our story is to stop telling ourselves disempowering ones." He also said that changing my story would "fuel lasting change."

Brené Brown said that the most powerful stories in our lives are the ones that we tell ourselves. My queen mothers from the lands of *Fix My Life* (Iyanla Vanzant) and *Live Your Best Life* (Auntie Oprah) spent hour after thoughtfully produced hour telling me how to own my story.

So clearly, I was living out a negative story of some kind and simply needed to tell myself a better, more positive one. Right?

Well, as much as I loved thinking of my life as a story that simply needed to be rewritten when it didn't seem like it was headed toward a happy ending, and as much as I really *do* believe in the power of thoughts to change your life, there was something that deeply bothered me about the simple way this idea was often presented. I had a feeling that there was more to the story (no pun intended). And that it ain't all my fault. (Or yours.)

At first glance, "stop telling yourself limiting stories" is a very empowering message—which is why it shows up over and over again. I even gave a speech once based on this very idea (not really understanding at the time how flawed it was). The "change the story you're telling yourself" advice is meant to encourage us to take responsibility for our own lives.

And what could be better than that? In fact, what could be more American? The directive falls very neatly in line with the rose-colored story of our country: a scrappy, upstart nation founded by pioneers who forged their own way and didn't let obstacles stop them from building a new world (an especially *lovely* story if you leave out all of the mass genocide, rape, and slavery parts). From that mythology, we inherited a culture of rugged, self-determined individualism. I mean, there's a reason why it's called "*self*-help." But thinking more deeply and critically on this advice, I just didn't buy it. It wasn't that I felt like I bore no responsibility whatsoever for my own unhappiness—I know that my mind is often filled with negative self-talk, my insecurities are sometimes crippling, and like any human, I am more than capable of less-than-perfect decision making. But the "it's all in your hands" idea seemed to be lacking something that I pride myself on not living or learning without: context.

Everyone wanted me to rush into taking responsibility like a fireman running into a fire without ever identifying the culprit or the cause of the blaze. In a 140-character, 6-sec video–driven world in which quotes and bullet-pointed ideas float around like autumn leaves blowing in the wind, we are perfectly comfortable accepting information and advice completely separate from the context from whence it came. But context is key. Context matters. Context is king.

Just as cherry-picking lines of sacred text from any religion without the cultural or historical context can lead you to create some shockingly ignorant justifications for prejudice and war, this kind of haiku life advice can lead to similar oversimplification.

"Let your work speak for itself" or "Move in silence, let success make the noise" sounds great, until you apply those maxims to a woman who has been routinely passed over for a raise and is afraid to advocate for herself.

"Don't look back, you're not going that way" sounds fantastic until you're mentoring someone who never stops to reflect or learn from his or her own mistakes.

"Fail fast, fail often" sounds great for the cool boys of Silicon Valley, but doesn't have quite the same ring to it when told to a single mom of two.

Advice without context is unhelpful at best, harmful at worst. And when it comes to how any human lives his or her life, there's a lot of context to look at. Unfortunately, many careers have been built off quick fixes, and self-empowerment thrives on listicles and sound bites, leaving little room for much nuance. That is the world in which "You wrote your story, just change it!" is presented as sufficient advice. That type of simplistic guidance has left a generation of people ill-prepared for the real world, which is getting more complex and dysfunctional by the day.

The gospel of "It's all up to you!" encourages a culture of navelgazing that distracts us from the world we say that we want to change. When we spend so much time looking at ourselves, our personal habits, our flaws, and what we're doing to cause our own pain, we never look up and take a break from wrestling with ourselves to analyze, critique, or just as passionately explore the world around us. We don't develop the language to push back against the systems and structures that harm us and make life so doggone hard. Or put another way, *we can't resist and destroy the forces that tie us up if we believe they are only in our heads.*

And so the Crooked Room Theory applies again. Summing up my problems by an admonition to write a new life story was like telling me to stand up straight without letting me know that the walls were slanted. How in the world was I supposed to fix my life if I didn't understand the world I was living in? How could I be satisfied with an explanation that said that the lack of fulfillment, the anxiety, frustration, and fear that I was feeling were all because of some negative self-talk and not enough positive storytelling?

To quote the great Rosa Parks when asked to move to the back of the bus, I say a loud and resounding "*Nah.*"

I was going to need deeper understanding of what the existing stories of my life were and how they worked in context.

WHAT'S INSIDE MY STORY?

When I was a little girl, I couldn't get enough of stories. They were like air to me: free, essential, and all around. I breathed them in, held them deep within my lungs until they seeped into my organs, and then, at the right moment, I exhaled them to anyone who would listen. When my parents would ask me after school how my day went, I would describe it in a series of dramatic stories, describing my classmates and teachers as characters and each event as an exciting plot point. "What stories do you have for me today, little girl?" my father would often ask.

Because I wasn't allowed to watch a lot of television, books were my favorite storytelling medium. Laura Ingalls Wilder, Nikki Giovanni, *Baby-Sitters Club*, Kahlil Gibran, my mother's tattered childhood collection of Nancy Drew mysteries, Zora Neale Hurston, Edgar Allan Poe, the *Essence* magazines stacked in the bathroom, the *Jet* magazines on my grandparents' coffee table, the *People* magazines in the doctors' offices. Then I'd hunt down books that were referenced inside of those books and magazines and read those too (which is why at twelve years old, I could recite Alfred Noyes's "The Highwayman" better than Anne of Green Gables ever could). I even attempted to read through the 1970s classic *Our Bodies, Ourselves* that I found in my mother's old box of books when I was seven. My grandmother found me before I got to the good parts with the sex drawings.

And don't get me started on the Bibles. Yes. I said Bibles with an "s." I was a pastor's kid; we had shelves and shelves of Bibles in our home. The NIV, the King James, the New King James, the Amplified, the Bible for Children (which had, of course, lots of pictures), the Bible for Women (which was, of course, pastel pink), the Bible for Black People (which had, of course, a kente cloth binding). I read through them all like I was studying for a final exam. Religious scholars can argue all they want about literal vs. figurative interpretations, but can't nobody tell me that the Bible, as literature, isn't a master class in storytelling. I marveled at the epic, miraculous narratives of my faith—the children of Israel breaking out of slavery, Jesus walking on water, the feeding of the five thousand. These stories were my daily bread. They would come alive every Sunday morning as my daddy told them from the pulpit. And they all taught powerful lessons, planting within me awe for an omnipotent God, one beyond comprehension and yet visible in the everyday magic and wonder of the human experience.

Even if you weren't reading Bibles for fun as a second grader, I guarantee that you were consuming some kind of stories. Maybe you watched a lot of TV. Cartoons. Movies. Comic books. Maybe you played video games. Maybe your mother read to you before bed. Or maybe you lived in the land of make-believe where stories were a dime a dozen, beautifully written and illustrated by your own imagination.

No matter how we shot it into our veins, most of us were addicted to stories by the time we could talk. How could we not be? Even outside of those books and shows, stories are everywhere. We are shoved out of our mothers' wombs into a world of stories that shape our lives.

These stories teach us how to live, who we are, what is possible, how the world works. When I talk about stories, though, I'm not just talking about the traditional "once upon a time" tales that we use to entertain ourselves. Stories are more than formalized dramas that people tell and consume. To me, "story" is a pattern or a paradigm, a way of processing information and experiences. I think of story as a narrative: the telling of particular facts in a way that reflects or conforms to an overarching set of aims or values. It's the connective tissue that strings together experiences, events, and even ideas in a narrative fashion to increase their meaning, memorability, and impact.

Stories have meaning packed inside of their DNA. And our minds are hardwired to process everything that we hear in that way. Our innate storytelling ability is one of the most powerful traits that separates us from all other animals. From the moment we are able to understand language, we understand the world through story and we begin to crave it. And by the time we are adults, we have been impacted and shaped by stories from multiple sources. I see them as falling into four different groups, each influencing us in a different way as we attempt to move and grow in the world.

THE FOUR TYPES OF STORIES

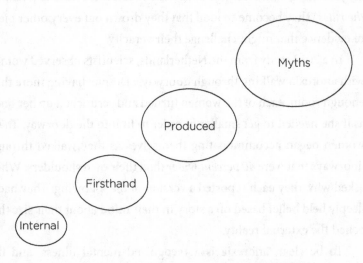

The Voices in My Head: aka Internal Stories

These are the stories that live inside of us, the ones with which self-help and psychology are largely preoccupied, and for good reason. They are the stories that we are most in control of (although it sometimes doesn't feel like it) because they live inside our own minds. They are the string of experiences and ideas that turn into beliefs echoing loudly between our ears as powerful thoughts. They are the stories on which we base our deepest, most private beliefs about ourselves and our lives. They guide our self-talk: the self-determined cans and can'ts, shoulds and shouldn'ts , dos and don'ts that provide a daily compass for our lives. They are the stories about our worth, about our potential, and our identity, where we fit in the world, what we deserve, and what our destiny holds.

Sometimes these internal stories are as quiet as a whisper, barely perceptible above the noise of the day, slipping into our thought processes and behaviors. But other times they are so loud and demanding that we actually speak them, bringing them into the world as fully formed ideas. These are stories like: *I am geeky not sexy. If I work hard, I will win. I can't function without structure. I am not my mother's favorite. If I talk too much, no one will like me. I have to follow all the rules.* They become so loud that they drown out every other piece of evidence that might challenge their veracity.

In a 2013 study from the Netherlands, scientists observed women with anorexia walking through doorways. Despite having more than enough room, each of the women turned and scrunched up her body as if she needed to get smaller in order to fit into the doorway. These women began accommodating themselves as they walked through doorways that were *40 percent wider* than their own shoulders. When asked why, they each reported a version of the following: They had a deeply held belief based on a story in their mind about their size that belied the external reality.

To be clear, anorexia is a recognized mental illness, and the resulting body dysmorphia is *far* more medically complicated than a simple storytelling conflict, but to my mind, this is a perfect illustration of how powerful internal stories can be.

The great Indian filmmaker Shekhar Kapur gave a TED Talk entitled, "We Are the Stories We Tell Ourselves." In it, he described a story as "the relationship between who you actually are, who you want to be, and the infinite world." He describes his creative process before making a film as intentionally throwing himself into chaos. On the first day of shooting, as he walks onto the set, he throws out his script and notes, abandoning everything that he planned to do and everything that he thinks that he knows to do in order to be panicked and access spontaneous truth. "Get out of your mind," he says, "because there is something outside of your mind that is greater, *more truthful than what is inside it.*"

What a jarring idea. The stories within our head that dictate to us what we think we know about ourselves, about what is possible, about what should be, may not in fact be true. Yet when they are told repeatedly and believed subconsciously—that is, without our awareness—they become so real that we move and contort ourselves in the real world accordingly. So it's no surprise that in many cases, these stories become self-fulfilling prophecies. And so it makes sense that when we are trying to identify the source of our own dissatisfaction, lack of progress, or even the source of society's greatest problems, we would first turn to the stories of how we see ourselves and move in the world.

If these questionable stories are indeed the strongest, as most motivational literature teaches, I would imagine that it is only because the voice that reads them to us day in and day out is our own. We trust that voice, we know that voice, and so ultimately, we believe that voice and the stories it tells.

But guess what? The fact that they are internal does not mean that we were *born with those specific stories.* We don't come into the world as babies with predetermined thoughts about how smart or capable or worthy we are, or about what our destiny should be. Even though they are in our heads now, they were developed by someone or something (or some ones or some things). The greatest challenge is to uncover where those stories actually come from. That's the hard work we're going to do together. If the stories that shape us are like Russian dolls, it is ineffective to try to get free by dealing only with the innermost stories. We have to work on the other layers as well.

I Saw, I Heard, I Felt: aka Firsthand Stories

When I was a little girl, a friend came over to my house for a sleepover, and I watched her spit into the toilet after brushing her teeth. I was horrified. Bougie child that I was, I had never in my life seen anyone spit into the toilet. I didn't want her to feel bad, but I had to let her know that this was wrong and I had to tell her why. I leaned over, held her hand, and said in the most earnest of ways, "We don't spit in the toilet here. *Because we're Christians.*" That's right. Somehow, I had made up a ridiculous story based on the myriad of other things that we didn't do as religious people (like curse, or listen to secular music) that spitting in the toilet was against my religion.

Remember how I said that our brain has an innate, almost automatic ability to process everything as a story? We desperately need to make sense of things so we use narrative as a connective tissue between otherwise disparate occurrences and things that we see or hear. These *firsthand stories* are the narratives and lessons that we believe as a result of something we have experienced, seen, or been told.

As humans in a "civilized" world, we crave order and meaning. So we create it, and are rewarded for it: Doing so often keeps us safe and identifies us as smart. When we look around us and pull data points from life, we want heroes and villains, clear beginnings and finite endings. We crave a sequential, page-by-page order. And above all, we always expect a *lesson.* We learn very early on that all good stories have a moral or a theme, some sort of instruction for living. Why would the world around us be any different? We are wired to see every action in the real world as a plot point, and every series of actions as a narrative arc with meaning and an instructive message. A parable, if you will.

For our young, impressionable minds (and even for our impressionable adult ones) real life is the greatest story ever told. We studiously consume what our parents and friends do, what our teachers and coaches say, the things that happen to us and to others around us. We take all of those components and force them into simple equations like A + B = C so that our stories make sense and have nice, neat lessons. *My sister ran on the ice. She fell and hurt herself. The moral of the story? Running on the ice is not a good idea.*

Firsthand stories are so vital to our everyday existence that an entire industry has been made of being voyeurs of others' lives. It's called social media. While one can argue that its higher purpose is to connect and communicate, in practice social media serves primarily as a way to observe as much as we possibly can about other people's lives in order to craft stories about them and, if we're honest, craft relative stories about ourselves based on what we see. It's as if we don't know who we are without seeing ourselves in relation to how others present themselves and their lives online.

Slowly but surely, these stories begin to shape our values and our identity. They shape what we believe, what we expect, and ultimately what we do. We develop stories about our age, gender, race, and sexual orientation. We develop stories about school and work, about money, success, and power. Before we know it, we have formed a worldview. And just as we avoided touching a stove after living or hearing a story about the danger of heat, our subsequent actions are, in one way or another, shaped by the stories we now believe.

But here's the problem with this mental storyboarding: We are rarely privy to the full context (there's that word again . . .) of any of the actions that we see and hear. Unlike a book with an omniscient narrator, or a movie with multiple perspectives, in real life we only glimpse the story that others let us see. We don't know that the guidance counselor told us that we'll never get into the school of our dreams simply because she was having a bad day. Or that our father hit our mother because he himself was abused as a child. Or that our married friends are posting romantic relationship-goals pictures of themselves to mask the fact that their marriage is on the verge of collapse. We don't know that our mother told us to dress a certain way, cover our bodies, not view ourselves as sexual beings, because she was sexually abused as a child and not because there is something inherently shameful or inappropriate about our bodies. Without curiosity, transparency, and perhaps some serious therapy, we make assumptions that become a part of who we are and how we see ourselves.

The truth about firsthand stories is that they rarely reveal the full truth, because it is so difficult to see what lies beyond our immediate circumstances or vantage point. So how can we orient ourselves in the world if not through things that we experience, see, and are told? They are important signposts that can and should be a part of how we navigate the world. But the lessons we pull from these stories should be more like hypotheses—*guesses* about life that need to be tested instead of held onto as gospel truths that we then build a life around, unchallenged and unquestioned; a life based on assumptions from incomplete stories written out of our painfully limited perspective of the world around us.

Once Upon a Time: aka Produced Stories

Produced stories are content intentionally created—usually by an identifiable author or creator—that was made for a specific purpose: to entertain, to comfort, to sell, to evoke a direct response. These are the TV shows, films, books, plays, songs, commercials, advertisements, billboards, PSAs, nonfiction forms like documentaries and testimonials and . . . everyone's favorite, the news. The length or medium isn't what defines these stories. The existence of an external creator with an intended goal is.

For those of you who work in politics, media, or advertising, what I'm about to say won't come as a shock. In fact, it will be like me saying, "water is wet." But for the rest of you, I've always wondered if you know just how many of the stories you consume are carefully tested, selected, engineered, designed, and edited to elicit a certain response from you. The answer: every single one of them.

Filmmaker Ken Burns famously said that "all story is manipulation." To manipulate is to change or control by artful or insidious means to serve one's purpose. So are they artful or insidious? I've seen both.

When I worked at Upworthy, our "manipulation" was for an admirable purpose. Sure, like any media company, we needed to ensure a certain number of clicks and views on our stories in order to sustain ad dollars and help us survive as a business. But the ultimate goal was always paramount: to tell stories that generated empathy, changed lives, and inspired people to actively do good in the world. The site used every bit of data it could to do this. We measured how long people read or viewed a piece of content, identified at what point in the story a viewer was lost, analyzed what words in the headlines made someone more likely to view the content in a certain way, created experiments that measured facial patterns as indicators of emotions, and conducted reader surveys on how each story made people feel. We paid attention to how the time of day impacted the types of stories being read, and how two different tones and voices telling the same story could make a difference. All of these findings were meticulously turned into best practices for how subsequent stories were created, so by the time the story ended up in your Facebook feed, we knew that we had done absolutely everything we could to make it touch you deeply and meet our end goal: uplifting you and inspiring you to think, feel, or behave in a more empathetic way.

In media, manipulation happens all the time. Diverse characters in books are cast as white or male in movies in order to appeal to a broader audience and make them more "relatable." The practice, called whitewashing, has happened since the beginning of film and continues today in the most egregious of ways: Tom Cruise playing what was originally a Japanese character in *Edge of Tomorrow* or Christian Bale playing an Egyptian in *Exodus: Gods and Kings*. The "real voters" chosen to tell their stories in political ads are hand-picked based on how their voice and their appearance "read" to the viewer. The endings of movies are market tested, not to see which one is objectively "better," but to see which one might make the audience feel just the right amount of satisfaction. (E.T. would have never ridden home on that bicycle if it weren't for this type of testing. The original version had him dying at the end.)

I'm telling you all of this because I want you to be conscious that all consumed stories have an author with a purpose—*and that author is not you*. And if that motive is anything other than to encourage your highest good, the stories themselves—and the lessons we pull from them about ourselves and the world—should be viewed with a critical eye. They must be taken with a grain (or two) of salt and curiosity. When we don't inquire about their origin and don't question the purpose of the narratives presented to us, we run the risk of adopting someone else's fantasies as truth and someone else's goals as our own.

The Big Ones: aka Cultural Myths

Take a deep breath and hold on to your seats for the reigning champion of the story world: cultural myths.

Cultural myths are the narratives that are most deeply ingrained in our psyches and, ironically enough, the stories that are the hardest to see. Myths are stories that teach us how the world works and how we all should live. They are seductive and powerful and tap into our deepest desires. These are ideas that are generations (if not centuries) old and inform our politics, the way our society is structured, and every other kind of story in our lives. They have deeper roots than *all* of the other stories—internal, firsthand, and produced.

Every single other story in our lives has formed either in alignment to or as a reaction to one of these myths. They are without question the most powerful stories we have. And they are, for the most part, habitually unquestioned.

Myths are the motivating stories or ideas behind common cultural practices. But let's be clear: *Calling something a myth does not make it inherently untrue.* It is simply a story or idea that explains the culture or customs of a people. Some of these cultural myths I find to be deeply problematic and harmful, while others I experience as wonderful ideals to strive toward that contradict reality, and others I choose to believe as true. That's right, there are actually cultural myths that I choose to believe 100 percent. The key word there is "choose." Cultural myths are the stories that often shape us without our consent, but in order to truly take control of our lives and change the world, it is up to us to decide which myths we choose to believe.

In American society, there are cultural myths around crime and punishment, identity, money and success, love, God, and humanity that provide the container for all of the other stories we see and consume. Most, if not all, of the myths are grounded in social, economic, and religious philosophies with very distinct points of view, like colonialism, capitalism, and monotheism.

Examples of cultural myths include:

- *The American Dream* A story of equal opportunity for prosperity, that in America hard work is a fair and accessible path to happiness and financial success.

- *A soul mate* The idea that there is one single person and one person only in this world of over X billion people that is meant for you, and that your goal in life is to find that person.

- *Meritocracy* The story that says that the best person—the most talented, most capable, smartest, strongest, most *deserving* in some way—always wins and gets ahead. This means that if someone has achieved something desirable it is because they have earned it.

- *Men must protect women* The patriarchal myth that men are necessarily the stronger protectors and women are inherently more sensitive, fragile beings in need of protection. This is why there was a ban on women in the military serving in combat . . . until *2013*.

As a person of faith, I am quite familiar with cultural myths. Encoding cultural myths is how religions were created and passed down. If I asked you what the story of the Bible is, you would probably say that the Bible is a book of stories. But a theologian would tell you that the Bible is actually one big cultural myth of God loving mankind and constantly trying to save us from some kind of eternal destruction. Every single story within the Bible is therefore shaped by this single narrative and springs from the following core premise: There is a God, God loves us and cares about our future, and we need God's guidance to survive. That framework and those basic assumptions from the myth of the Big Story are what all of the other stories within are built upon. But if you don't believe that, the individual stories may not hold up either.

All of the things we see, hear, buy, and ultimately believe—every single other story that shapes our lives—exists within broader Big Stories that shape the systems of the world around us. They are the beams of our room, whether crooked or straight.

THE POWER OF STORY

Any of these stories told well or often enough can convince us of just about *anything*. Stories shape our feelings, our expectations, and our desires, not to mention our day-to-day choices. They even shape our sense of self and identity. We both discover and become who we are based on the stories that help us make sense of the world and our place in it.

You know who really understood this? Plato. "Then we must first of all, it seems, supervise the storytellers," he said. "We'll select their stories whenever they are fine and beautiful and reject them when they aren't. And we'll persuade nurses and mothers to tell their children the ones we have selected, since they will shape their children's souls with stories much more than they will shape their bodies by handling them."

That's why the role of the storyteller is, has always been, and will always be so highly prized. In West African culture, the griot—the traveling storyteller and musician—isn't an important figure simply because stories are entertaining. He or she is considered the keeper of wisdom, the shaper of lives and history, the owner of the culture. Philosopher Alasdaire MacIntyre once said, "I can only answer the question 'What am I to do?' if I can answer the prior question, 'Of what story or stories do I find myself a part?'"

The Co-Intelligence Institute has studied how transformation of any kind—psychological, organizational, or social—is usually preceded or accompanied by a change in the stories that govern that system. In other words, major life change is always connected to changing your story. If only doing so were easy. Unfortunately, it's not.

NOW YOU SEE IT, NOW YOU DON'T

Here's the catch: The power of stories lies largely in their invisibility. And that's what makes changing stories and discovering the truth so darn hard. I have just laid out, in great detail, the types of stories that shape our world, and so it is, right in this moment, very easy to identify them. But that is not so in our day-to-day lives. As with molecules, just because you know they are there doesn't mean you can see them. The stories that form our beliefs and values and options exist without us even seeing them and without us realizing their intent or effect. Oftentimes, we would reject them outright if we did.

For example, who would ever believe statements like "A woman is only valuable if she has a man" or "A person with dark skin is inherently evil"? Our evolved brain must know the reasons why each of these statements is false. (If yours doesn't, you may want to put this book down, back away, and we can pretend this whole conversation never happened . . .)

More than likely, no one has said those exact words to you. Instead, countless versions of internal, firsthand, and consumed stories, as well as cultural myths, have shaped us so that the first question we wonder about a woman is whether or not she is married, and the first, instinctual response that many people have when they see a dark-skinned man walk down the street is to lock their car doors or hold their purses. We have been manipulated to believe these stories. The particular phenomenon of how we perceive others based on their identity is called *implicit bias*, but it holds true for any subconscious manipulating of our thoughts and behaviors. This is why I know that story is one of the most effective "power tools" known to man and always has been. And that poses a unique problem for our generation.

WE LIVE IN
THE WILD, WILD WEST OF STORIES

Although most of us don't know it, the story tug-of-war is what is currently bringing us in droves to a life-altering crossroads of ambition, dissatisfaction, and confusion. Epic tales about who we are and how we should live are competing for dominance in our minds and hearts every second of every day. Each story comes with its own lessons, its own ideas, and its own legitimate reason for being. Each of them seems believable . . . and so we believe. Most of our lives are spent vacillating between stories, trying to make decisions and lead our "best lives." I know this because we are the guinea pigs of marketing, more than any generation before.

Capitalism, the internet, social media, reality TV—the intensity and prevalence of these warring stories practically force us to absorb messages that scream: "Let me tell you who you are and what you should be doing, thinking, desiring, buying, and believing." Tack on the ever-green influences of education, politics, culture, and family, and many of us today find ourselves overwhelmed, leading lives that were shaped by everyone and everything but our own pure internal compasses.

And while the war of stories is probably as old as time itself—every society has lived its own myths while every generation has pushed and pulled against them—there are two realities that make our current story landscape a truly difficult one to navigate:

1. There are more stories now than ever. The minute that we open our eyes in the morning, we are assaulted by stories. Messages and advertisements and images and ideas of what we should be and how the world works are everywhere we turn. We are advertised to on billboards, on the backs of airplane seats, in the backseat of cabs, and even on refrigerator doors. We share our stories and consume the stories of others through social media. And we consume more content a day than previous generations thought was scientifically possible. In fact, it's estimated that the average person devotes more than ten hours a day to screen time. And each of those stories is on a mission, determined to be seen, heard, and believed.

My colleague and friend, former *New York Times* journalist Amy O'Leary, said it best when discussing the current landscape: "We [as content creators] are in a street fight for attention and story is our weapon." Thanks to the internet, stories about love are no longer just coming from fairy tales and movies and the relationships we see around us, but also from #relationshipgoals and dating apps and any URL that includes the letters "XXX." Stories about education aren't just coming from parents, educators, and politicians but also from YouTube experts and celebrities who are launching schools and for-profit colleges that run pop-up ads on your favorite YouTube expert's channel. Stories about our bodies no longer just come from our families, our doctors, and commercials and movies. They are also coming from the diet industry, which is paying Photoshopped models and filtered Instagram influencers to pitch us weight loss teas and appetite suppressant lollipops—these aren't just celebrities, mind you. Now it's "everyday people" being paid to tell us believable yet wholly untrue tales about tooth whiteners and waist trainers in the midst of their stories about going to school and being a working mom.

If being bombarded isn't bad enough, the underlying narratives themselves are often conflicting. On one hand, we consume what I like to call the "fantasy" stories: the ones that support a pervasive utopian narrative that, unlike our parents and grandparents, our generation can truly have it all. We can be well educated, entrepreneurial, beautiful, "woke," masters of capital, well traveled, creative, fit and athletic, vegan, and spiritually aligned—all of that just by being born when we were born. Our Instagram, Twitter, and Facebook feeds reassure us that everyone around us is living their dream, wearing cute vintage clothes, having babies, buying homes, starting tech-based businesses, and feeding children in Africa (not a specific country, of course, just the continent) via their sustainably sourced cell phones, all while competing in CrossFit competitions and growing perfect, healthy hair. These fantasy stories are like balloons pulling us high into the clouds, creating the contours of our own dreams and goals for which we are constantly striving.

But if you've ever felt that those balloons were unimaginably out of reach, that all of the fantasy stories can never apply to you, you probably have "fact" stories to blame. Fact stories are the narratives on the other end of the spectrum that pull us emotionally and psychologically underground like two-ton weights. They are the pins to our bubbles. Every day there is new data, a new poll, shouting a depressing and frightening statistic about our present and future.

These stories create a narrative of lack and insufficiency and point to data as the ultimate predictor of possibility and destiny. They encourage us to paint a picture using only the odds.

The *odds* are that if you are a young black male under the age of twenty-five from a certain neighborhood, you are more likely to be killed or wind up in jail than graduate from college. (According to the National Bureau of Economic Research, the homicide rate among fifteen to twenty-four-year-old black males is eighteen times higher than it is for white men of the same age. And black men as a whole are six times as likely as white men to be incarcerated.) The *odds* are that if you are a woman, you will never reach beyond a certain position of leadership in corporate America. (According to the Catalyst research group, only about 5 percent of Fortune 500 companies have female CEOs and just 21 percent of their board seats are held by women.)

And according to Pew Research and the *Financial Times*, the *odds* are that if you are a millennial, you will be far worse off economically than your parents at the same age.

As a result of those fact-based stories, it would be easy to believe that things are hopeless and that trying to win anything in a way that is aligned with your values and allows you to be your authentic self is a fruitless, futile endeavor. We begin to be haunted by a nagging feeling that we are small and limited, unable to achieve greatness because of forces that threaten to consume us: our backgrounds, racism, sexism, homophobia, the economic environment, lack of resources, amount of debt, insufficient education . . . whatever the perceived inadequacy is (or whatever the very real structural barrier is that society has placed in front of us), we believe that we are doomed: ill-equipped to climb the mountain, fight the obstacle, impact the system, slay the giant, and live an epic life.

2. There are fewer gatekeepers, filters, and guides than ever. I asked my baby boomer mother who it was that helped her learn about life, and her response was quick: her parents, her teachers, and her peers. Throw in the traditional gatekeepers of journalism and government, and "voilà!"—here were the people and institutions that were designed to assist my mother in developing a life road map and finding her place in the world. Were they always right? Of course not. Were they undoubtedly motivated by their own interests and stories as well? Absolutely.

But our current world has seen the pendulum swing as far to the other side as it can. Many of those same institutions have either entirely collapsed or are no longer trustworthy. The freedom of information and access to it, coupled with the disintegration of journalism, the corruption of politics, the diminishing quality of public education, and the irrelevance and stagnation of traditional religious institutions have left us all swinging in the wind, attempting to craft a worldview and an identity based on an unlimited supply of uncurated stories and actual fake news. We are unprotected from the onslaught of stories and unaided in our journey through the battle. And that is why we are so painfully vulnerable to the power of story, now more than ever.

Realizing all of this left me feeling bamboozled and hoodwinked. It started to hit me just how little agency I had exercised in determining what I believed to be true about myself, my life, and the world around me. As a political strategist, a media maker, and an armchair theologian, I had spent most of my life telling stories meant to change the world and help people live better lives, and yet I had somehow failed to realize just how much of a slave I had become to those very same stories, giving no thought as to whether the impact was positive or negative.

It was suddenly so clear what I must do. I would pull apart the tangled narrative web that had been strung together over my lifetime, story by powerful story.

CHAPTER 3

GETTING STORY SMART

During Kanye West's ill-fated 2018 return to Twitter, the one in which he called slavery a choice and professed his love for Donald Trump, he posted a quote commonly misattributed to Harriet Tubman. "I could have freed a thousand more if only they knew they were slaves."

The public promptly corrected and mocked him, letting him know that despite its presence on hundreds of memes, Harriet Tubman never, ever said those words. The quote was completely made up and often used in the same harmful way that he had used it: to blame a people for their own oppression.

But I have a shameful confession to make, one that I would have made then if I weren't myself a dues-paying member of the Woke Internet: I too had thought she said those words. I'd heard the quote time and time again. And the lesson that *I* had always taken from it— although clearly not the one that West had intended to convey—was one that I wholeheartedly believed: *freedom depends on awareness*; recognition is the prerequisite for liberation.

How can we ever hope to break free from the crooked room and rewrite the stories of our lives if we don't clearly recognize the stories we erroneously believe? Better yet, if we can't identify the stories that have turned our world into the hot mess that it is, how can we ever clean it up?

Many of us walk around in a constant state of bondage, held hostage by the powerful stories that have taught us how the world, presumably, works. But why is that? Why do we believe these stories without objection, so wholeheartedly and unconsciously?

Because we were never taught any other way. Most of us were taught to be some combination of book smart and street smart; to take facts, information, and education, add some reason and common sense, pour in two cups water, mix together, and like magic, we would be smart! This concoction is what we think of when we think of traditional *intelligence*. We know that without a modicum of it, life would be impossibly hard. So we are programmed to learn the information and skills that others have told us are necessary for survival, believing that doing so will help us make good decisions and move through the world successfully. Isn't that what school *and* the internet are all about?

Some of us were lucky enough to learn to be people smart too; to understand and connect to emotions in ourselves and in others. That's called *emotional intelligence*. Without it, we have a hard time engaging effectively with the people around us, building relationships, and managing our own internal life. So unless we've been living under a rock and never interacting with other humans, we are often taught to actively practice our emotional intelligence skills every chance we get.

And that's where the typical life lessons end. Reading, writing, arithmetic, and social skills. Yet there's one glaring omission: We are never taught how to be story smart; how to recognize and understand the stories that are at play in our lives, so that we can make these stories work *for* us, not against us. I call this skill *narrative intelligence*.

The term itself isn't new. In media and technology studies, the concept is defined as "the tendency that our brain has to process information through story." But in my definition, narrative intelligence isn't just the ability to process information but also the *ability to see and respond to the stories that shape us, adopt the ones that are helpful*, and *discard the toxic or harmful ones.*

To describe narrative intelligence using painfully overused pop culture language, it's all about being "woke." Here, I mean it in the original, black vernacular use of the term: an actual awakening or a perceived awareness. To have a high level of narrative intelligence is to be woke enough to recognize the messages and stories that we are exposed to and *then make a choice* to actively respond to them—either by consciously embracing them or rejecting and replacing them with new stories that can serve us better.

Now that I think about it, narrative intelligence is what us church folks call *discernment*. In religious terminology, *discernment* is the ability to see beyond what is visible to the naked eye in order to make wise and God-inspired choices. Without it, we can easily fall victim to the limited vantage point of our own eyes and make decisions without understanding the greater spiritual context. Narrative intelligence also helps us see stories beyond what is visible to the naked eye, in order to make wise, inspired choices for our lives. Without it, we will continue to make decisions, big and small, without understanding the greater narrative context. With it, we'll be story smart; we'll recognize the underlying context in which we're living, and be able to make informed decisions that will help us reach our goals.

WHAT HAPPENS
WITHOUT STORY SMARTS

To show you what can happen without narrative intelligence, let me give you two examples. One individual and one societal. Just for fun, we'll start on the macro level, and work our way down. You can take the girl out of politics, but you can't take politics out of the girl, so humor me and take a look at our current political climate as our first case study.

American Horror Story

In 2008, America voted for "change" in the historic election of Barack Obama. By doing so, we essentially wrote a new story; we arrived at a dramatic, inspiring new chapter in American history that we hoped would be the realization of our highest aspirations, deepest values, and wildest dreams. "Hooray! We are post-racial!" America said. "We aren't red or blue, we are one! And we are moving forward!"

We were so excited about this new story that we slapped it on bumper stickers, T-shirts, brick walls in Brooklyn. All around the world, the story was being told about America's great change, embodied by our singular triumph: electing a black man to the highest office in the land.

For the next *eight years*, we told this story over and over and over again. We held on to it tightly, despite mass shootings, hate crimes, police brutality, the rapid expansion of the prison system, the shrinking of the news media, the rise of the Tea Party, an obstructionist and angry Congress, and the highest number of immigrant raids and deportations in American history. We repeated our story so often that our hopes morphed into a delusional belief: that the tide had turned for good, and all of these other negative stories were just blips on the screen. None of those horrible realities mattered as much as the story of our new America.

It's not that Obama's election wasn't historic, symbolic, inspiring, and meaningful. It was. The problem was that it became our *single* story. And people who wanted to desperately believe in everything that story represented ignored the other signs that we as a nation were in deep, deep trouble.

Writer Chimamanda Ngozi Adichie warned us of the danger of a single story in her now famous 2009 TED Talk. She recognized that holding on to a single, powerful story often blinds us to other critical truths about a person or place. In her example, when we believe in a singular narrative that a certain place is "poor," like the story of Africa that is most often told in the West, we miss all of the other truths about that place: That Africa is also the continent richest in natural resources. That Africa is the birthplace of civilization. That Africa has a long and diverse history and culture, thriving business communities, emerging markets, and so much else to offer. The single story of Africa as poor shapes how we view the people who live there and, in turn, can lead us to wholly inaccurate assumptions about everything, including our own position in the world.

A rabid adherence to one narrative to the exclusion of all others guarantees a fundamental miscalculation of the reality. To focus on one single story is a serious lack of narrative intelligence; it means being ignorant of the many stories that exist, and not knowing how the narrative you cling to actually impacts your day-to-day reality and decisions.

So despite evidence presenting itself every single day that America was not a utopian post-racial, forward-thinking, and wholly united land of lilies and MLK dreams, many of us believed the Obama narrative so deeply that we ignored any and everything that challenged that idea. Then came Election Day 2016: a reality check that kicked us in the collective ass.

I woke up on November 9 and pulled the covers over my head, afraid to move. Maybe if I just stayed still for a while, I would discover the previous night's election results had been a part of some really vivid nightmare. But it wasn't a fever dream. A reality TV star who had bragged about grabbing pussy, who had expressed a proud hatred for immigrants, Muslims, and black people, a white supremacist Twitter bully who had never held any political office and had zero qualifications to run our country would now be making decisions that impacted my life and the lives of my loved ones for generations to come.

"How could this have happened?" we cried. "What happened to our story of change?"

Well, everyone and their mama had an answer: fake news, racism, reality TV, the economy, sexism, the internet, the failure of the media, the class divide, coastal elitism, and on and on and on. And frankly, all of those explanations ring true if all you're seeking is blame. But if we see each of these issues as its own story, its own narrative unfolding every day across America, the problem becomes a little clearer: Those of us who were more excited by the prospect of forward progress than we were afraid of it were not using our narrative intelligence.

We had failed to pay attention to the world of stories that surrounded our one, single fairy tale. Our story of hope and change had essentially been beaten within an inch of its life by all the other stories—historical and present-day—that we had ignored. And the powerful stories that many didn't see and others chose to ignore were the stories that exposed just how much work still had to be done and how truly fragile our newfound change was.

Had we exercised some story smarts and examined the *context* in which Obama won and led—where government was still broken, where people still felt unrepresented and were still struggling, and where -isms and phobias of all kinds still existed—we would have seen how so many Americans found those other stories so powerful. As it turns out, most of them were actively working *against* the story of hope and change we so desperately wanted to be true.

If we had paid as much attention to all of these stories, and invested ourselves more deeply in countering those narratives, perhaps we might have been better prepared for what eventually happened: A candidate arrived on the scene who was able to personify and validate the dangerous stories of division, anger, greed, and fear. By giving those stories a platform, he awakened their power to change the world just as powerfully as Obama's story of hope and change had.

Hindsight is, of course, 20/20. In the aftermath, day after day, the battle of stories wages on, each side trying to scream the simplest, shallowest narrative about who and what America really is and should be, and neither side taking the time to effectively articulate and deconstruct the broader cultural stories about power, leadership, money, and race that continue to shape this country. So the madness continues. And that, my friend, is what it looks like when an entire country doesn't have story smarts.

In my humble opinion, it's going to take an uprising of story-smart voices to right this ship. We need leaders who can recognize and then address our deeply ingrained cultural narratives and provide a vision based on entirely new stories. Only then will we be able to collectively write a new story together. And just maybe those leaders are you and me.

And speaking of you and me . . . let's bring this big idea back down to our individual lives.

The Self-Help Trap

Let's say that you wake up one morning and decide, *I am now a vegetarian.* That story is new and exciting, so you spend the day reading everything that supports it—blogs about poorly treated animals and ethics, and why vegetarianism is the way to better health, a better body, a better world. You're loving this new story and you momentarily forget, or don't pay attention to, all the stories that created your *context.*

You forgot that you have heard your entire life that a complete meal includes a meat and two sides. You didn't realize how much you believe that meat is the best, if not only, source of essential protein. You didn't remember the story about your grandfather's famous fried chicken, and how that and all the other meat-based soul food your family enjoys has been passed down for generations, and is a large part of your cultural identity. But all those stories are rattling around in your brain, just pushed to the side.

By the time dinner rolls around, you have no idea how to reconcile your new story ("I don't eat meat") with the competing stories that are burned into your brain. By 7:30 p.m., you are in a panic, worried that you won't have enough protein in your diet, questioning whether or not you can make a complete meal and how you're going to relate to your family. By 8:15 p.m., you're tossing a pack of hot dogs in the oven and stirring bacon baked beans on the stove. Those older stories (and your own lack of narrative intelligence) did your planning in.

That competition cycle plays out over and over again in each of our meaningful moments of transition—big and small. We read the self-help books, write the New Year's resolutions, get the degrees, fast and pray, launch the new projects, quit the jobs or start new ones, and immediately begin reciting our own little story that we desperately want to believe about who we are now. We say our story mantras:

I am a full-time creative.

I will have the relationship of my dreams.

I am successful.

I am, I can, I will [fill in the blank with your aspirations].

Because we've been taught the story that we can do, be, or have anything (but weren't really told how to get it), we believe wholeheartedly in our new story and charge into the world to create a new life. The cultural ideal of self-determination empowers us to be the captain of our ship, heading into any storm, believing that with a little bit of grit and elbow grease, we can do *anything*. But without narrative intelligence, we pay no attention to the other stories that have shaped us and are connected, like blood vessels, to the heart of our new story.

Without recognizing and responding to the stories that impact the vision you have for your new life or who you want to be in the world, eventually your new story will collapse, taking you down with it. This is the cycle we engage in, running from one new endeavor, commitment, or dream to the next, working hard to take control of our lives and stand up straight, only to find ourselves forever crooked. This is the reason why so many of us, including me, work so hard and yet don't feel as if we have made the transformation we set out to make.

Well it's time to break the cycle. We do not have to be puppets on invisible strings, dancing through life trying to make choices but unknowingly being pulled to and fro by the power of story. Narrative intelligence wakes us up, helps us see the strings, and gives us the power to cut the ones that are moving us in the wrong direction or, worse, keeping us stuck in the same position.

Perhaps you too are in a moment of transition or transformation, trying to move to a new level of focus, clarity, or impact. If so, you are exactly where I was several years ago. And I'll say to you what I said to myself then:

On the journey to build a bold, beautiful life and world, I refuse to be a casualty of the war of stories. I want to face every decision and challenge in my life—from my career path to my religious beliefs to my politics—with a clear-eyed understanding of why I do what I do and want what I want. Turning points or questions in my life will be met with a confidence that says, "Here are my

*values, and here is the story that I believe about my potential
and path. I will line up with those values, no matter what else."*

Make the power of story work for you, not against you. It's time
to get story smart.

GET STORY SMART

For most of my life, I was ignorant of the stories and context that had
shaped my decisions, hopes, and dreams and had no idea how to write
new stories, stories that were better and more true. To remedy that, I
needed to take a long, hard look at the major stories that had shaped me
(and in some cases, my generation) to figure out the narratives that would
lead me to the life I knew I deserved—and the world that I dreamed of.

Getting to that point of self-determination, where I consciously
chose the most powerful stories in my life to create lasting change,
was going to be a process. First came *awareness*: recognizing the stories at play. Then *understanding*: knowing how these stories impacted
my life, whether positively or negatively. Next, *response*: making a
choice to either embrace the story or reject it and create a new one.
And finally the practice and work toward *mastery*: behaving in a way
that made the power of story work in my favor.

As simple as that.

To work through that process, I was going to have to figure out a
practice, an easy-to-remember and easy-to-share method that could
help me habitually exercise my story smart muscle. So I came up with
a set of four questions to ask myself whenever I was confronted with
a new story.

These questions would be my guide. They would help me take an
honest look at my life and begin to identify the narratives, the deeply
held beliefs about identity, purpose, and the world that had shaped

my current reality (which, at the time, was jobless, disillusioned, and, for the most part, lost). These would be the four questions that would take me on a journey from awareness and understanding of the stories that held me back to response and mastery of new stories that served me.

QUESTION 1: What is the story?
(Awareness)

Pause from the routine of your life and acknowledge the otherwise invisible.

So much power lies in this simple question, it's like the Pringles of questions: Once you start, you can't stop. Asking, "What is the story?" almost always begets asking another question, and another, and then yet another. The initial question is the start of the great unraveling that helps you get to the heart of the matter.

- What do I believe about this topic?

- Who taught me that?

- Who created this story and why?

- Where in my life or in the world have I seen it?

- Where do my ideas around this topic come from?

- My beliefs, fears, assumptions, and certainties about this topic are based on what premise?

- What else has to be true in order for this story to be true?

- What is the context for this story?

- If I were writing a children's book about this topic, what would the moral of the story be?

Let's take a superficial, seemingly harmless example to illustrate the point. For most of my life, I had long, thick, healthy hair. It was, as they say, my crowning glory. And I thought about it obsessively. I made decisions about social activities based on how the environment and timing would impact my hair: How soon can I get a hair appointment? Will it be raining? How many days can I keep the style if I don't work out?

Then one day I'd had enough. I didn't want to live like that—catering to the weather and my hair's response—anymore. India.Arie sang years ago "I am not my hair," so I knew that I had to stop being a slave to the power that my hair had over me.

So I thought, *Question: What's the story here?*

Answer: My hair is the prettiest thing about me.

Wow. Okay. That seems simple (and yet profound) enough.

But I kept digging.

- Why do I believe that?

- Who taught me that?

- What are the indicators that I'm using to determine that?

- What do I see as pretty?

- What story have I believed about my hair?

The answers came up fast. "My grandmother and father always bragged about my hair and told me never to have it messy." And "Well, long hair is just more feminine and if it doesn't look long and thick and healthy, I'll look masculine and, because I'm tall, I think looking more masculine makes me look like a WNBA player and then I won't be cute." And "The thing that makes me special is my hair. Will anyone think I'm special if my hair isn't beautiful?" The final answer: *The story here is that my identity as a woman is hugely impacted by how others perceive my physical beauty. My self-esteem is determined by how beautiful others think I am.* Boom. There's the core story at play between me and my hair.

I could trace it from my internal story (I need my hair to be perfect at all times) to a consumed story (perfect hair is thick and long, and thick and long hair is feminine) all the way up to a cultural myth (my femininity is connected to my desirability and women are made to be beautiful). My hair is my worth.

With statements as bold and clear as those, I saw the immediate separation between that story (which had shaped so many of my behaviors) and my values. And living out of alignment with one's values is a surefire recipe for discontent.

Whatever the core story is that you end up with, say it out loud and write it down without judgment. Make it plain, no equivocation, so that it sounds almost harsh and overly simplistic to your own ears. That's the only way to recognize its power. Once that happens, look back to see where it came from, and become aware of wherever that story plays out in your life. Pinpoint everywhere this core story presents itself. I paid attention to every time during the week that I thought about my hair, made a decision based on my hair, chose my hair over something else—like fun or sleep—and took note of just how often this story had impacted my life, in ways that I hadn't even realized.

Once you do that, then you're ready to tackle Question #2.

QUESTION 2: Does this story serve my values and me?
(Understanding)

Once you've identified the story (or stories) that are underlying your decisions and beliefs in a certain area, it's time to ask yourself the most clarifying question of all. It requires an honest look at your life. *Does this story serve my values and me?*

When you make decisions based on the premise of the story, what is the outcome? Does it benefit someone else—perhaps the creators and the promoters of the story—far more than it benefits you? Has this story helped you make what the writer Kiese Laymon calls "loving, healthy choices"—choices that help you thrive and lead you toward true wholeness? Does it align with what you say matters most, or does it conflict with what you truly believe about life?

So many times, the tension we feel between our ideals and our actual lived experience comes from this misalignment of values or the conflict it creates. Here, evaluate the concrete results of your life, as well as your feelings about those results. Feelings, while not always a foolproof indicator of right and wrong, can be a useful tool to measure the overall impact of a story.

- How has believing this story made you feel, more often than not?

- Can you see any harm that it has caused you?

- Has this story caused more pain than gain? Or more gain than pain?

- Has it brought you closer to the person that you want to be, the life that you want to create, and the world that you want to live in? Or has it taken you further away from those ideals?

Oftentimes, the stories that we automatically believe—you know, the ones that appear without any sort of context—are either pushing us toward an unhealthy goal or are holding us back from a beneficial one. In my hair example, the story about the importance of my physical beauty and attractiveness wasn't serving me. That story reduced me to other people's opinions, not to mention that it took up entirely too much mental space.

Once you answer Question #2 and have understood the role and impact of the story, you have only two options: accept the story, or reject and replace it.

Either way, you must respond to it.

QUESTION 3: What if I believed something else?
(Response)

If the answers to Question #2 led you to accept this story that has shaped you, congratulations! There isn't much work left for you to do. You've seen the story, you've understood the role it plays in your life, and you have decided that it aligns with your values.

But if not, here comes the fun part. Or the scary part. If you're clear that your core story isn't serving you, it's time to imagine a new one that can. And the best way to try to see outside of what you've always seen or been told is to ask a simple but potentially ground-breaking question: *What if?*

• What if you believed something different?

• What if you adopted another story?

Asking *what if* gives us an opportunity to explore alternative stories; new ways of thinking, working, fighting, dreaming, and living that may be better suited to what we value. In fact, some of the biggest scientific and cultural breakthroughs in history have started with that very question.

"What if the Earth isn't flat?" "What if we could get from point A to point B without actually walking?" "What if white and black people had the same opportunities, learned in the same classroom, or ate at the same lunch counter?"

So it makes sense that major breakthroughs in your life and worldview would begin that way as well. "What if I didn't do things the same way that my parents did?" "What if I decided to create a new kind of family?" "What if I built a career in which money wasn't the ultimate goal?"

"What if" is always my favorite part of the process. I can spend hours contemplating my "what ifs." So when I was thinking through the drama that was my hair, I what if'ed away. *What if my hair was less than "perfect"? What if I didn't have this hair at all? Would I still be special? Would I still be beautiful?*

Now, let's be clear. As easy as this sounds, shaking the foundation of the stories you've believed—some since childhood—can be a painful, scary process. The vulnerability, humility, and courage that it takes to imagine new ways of thinking, being, and seeing cannot be understated. It can be messy and emotional; it can take a long time; it can require shifts in multiple areas of your life; it can come as a surprise to the people around you; it can occur at a cost. But the work is worth the effort.

QUESTION 4: What can this new story look like for me?
(Mastery)

Once you land on a new story, it's time to make it work for you. Narrative intelligence is ultimately about making real choices and changing behaviors to make your life and the world better. Ask yourself, "Where in my life can I begin putting this new story to the test?" It's time to start practicing.

I use the word "practice" here in two ways. First, practice as a verb means the repetition of something in order to prepare for a big, higher stakes moment when we really need the skill. That is what we must do with our new stories: create ways to test and prove them every single day, even in ways small and unimportant, so that when we are in need of them for a major decision or moment, we are ready.

Once I had my new story—how I look on the outside is irrelevant to everything that really matters to me—I would do small, seemingly insignificant things all the time to confirm it, like not wear lip gloss when leaving the house, or take pictures for Instagram even if my hair wasn't freshly styled. I would film videos for my business even if I hadn't gotten my makeup professionally done. I started experimenting with colors and clothing styles that I would never have chosen before because they weren't "flattering." I wore *sweat pants in public*. Were any of these life-altering behaviors? Of course not. In hindsight, they sound downright silly. But they really helped me exercise my new story muscle.

And then one day, I cut all my hair off. I sat in the hairstylist's chair and let my tears fall to the floor along with my thick, cottony-soft locks and thought, *Well, now you have no excuse. You're gonna learn to think of yourself as beautiful now no matter what.* And I did. I'm glad I did it. It's since grown back, but I'll never forget the power of learning how to appreciate myself with short hair.

I also use the word "practice" as a noun, like a yoga practice or a spiritual practice, a discipline of regular actions or activities to cultivate development. The practice of recognizing an unhelpful story and its sources and replacing it with a new story is how narrative intelligence moves from a task to a habit and, ultimately, to creating our default way of looking at the world. It is a discipline that should be a part of our daily lives.

As a religious person, I am drawn to the idea of ritual. A ritual is a sacred act, performed with diligence, determination, humility, and commitment. Carl Jung talked about how during his encounter with Pueblo Indians, he discovered their belief that their rituals literally made the sun rise every day. He quoted one of the indigenous people he met as saying, "We do this not only for ourselves, but for the world. If we were to ease practicing our religion, in ten years' time the sun would no longer rise. Then it would be night forever."

I believe the same is true of the big and small ways that we practice rejecting and rewriting harmful stories. The practice of rejecting old stories and believing in new ones is a true ritual of resistance. And it is a ritual that we must do every day, in big and small ways, so that the sun can rise on the world that we want to create.

The good news is that your beautiful new story doesn't just have to come from your imagination. Do some basic research—begin asking others what they believe, what story guides their thinking. Look for other people who practice and believe something different than you do. Not only are human experiences the best way to understand new ideas, but this process will also help you feel less alone.

That said, if there's no one you know that you feel comfortable talking to about the new story (which is often the case, especially if everyone around you believes the same bad story), typing away with good old Google doesn't hurt. Thanks to the internet, we have access to ideas, lifestyles, models, and approaches to just about everything under the still-rising sun.

Finding ways to search for, pursue, act out, and share new stories daily serves the ultimate goal: to *change* the old ones, to use our narrative intelligence every chance we get so that it becomes our default posture. This is how we will prevail over all of the other narratives that try to define us. That is how we will tear down the crooked walls.

And that, my loves, is how we transform.

BRINGING IT ALL TOGETHER

I wish I could tell you exactly which stories aren't serving you, which narratives have held your mind captive, holding you back from being the fulfilled, free, and focused world-changer I know you can be. All I can do is tell you what worked for me. In the rest of this book, I'm going to show you what happened when I applied this principle and these questions to my life.

Some of these stories represent areas in which you too may have struggled. They are the areas where powerful stories have bombarded all our lives on a day-to-day basis. And while the following stories are very personal to my own journey, they are examples of what it looks like to move, bit by bit, exercising narrative intelligence and creating that beautiful image that was my father's last: a powerful new life.

The rest of this book is a look at the seven stories that were integral on my journey to new life.

I focus on these seven for a few reasons. First, they were the stories that I wrestled with the most and that had the most dramatic results. Secondly, they are culturally relevant—I see them in the lives of my peers, colleagues, mentees, even the strangers who email me and come up to me after talks, nearly every day. And I am willing to bet that they are the key narratives that have shaped your life as well.

A WORD OF ADVICE: A NEW PATH

There will be a tendency as you go through this book—and your life—to look for a straightforward new path. That is certainly how I began my journey. If you're anything like me, you will be excitedly hoping that if you put one foot in front of the other, a clear paved road to a better life will suddenly and magically appear. You may even be tempted to look at my story or the stories of others in the book as success stories to follow to a T. I have certainly looked at others this way. This desire is natural.

The path that we were told *would* work—do good in school, get a good job, make great money, find the perfect partner, have kids, and live happily ever after—perhaps hasn't worked out exactly the way we thought it would. Or even if it did, maybe it didn't *feel* the way that we assumed it would emotionally and spiritually. So we turn to books and celebrity profiles and gurus for a different path, the *right path*, with step-by-step directions to get us from point A to point Z.

This desire itself is shaped by a powerful meta story that most of us have consumed since childhood: the story that there is a single right path that we have to find and follow. So we go through life looking for our very own yellow brick road. For those of us who consider ourselves either ambitious or dreamers, obsessed with doing the right and best thing, much time is spent looking for the path that we are supposed to be on to get us where we are trying to go. We walk around our lives in the dark with flashlights, hoping to stumble upon a straight and narrow way that is predetermined, that others before us have followed and can tell us about, the road that can move us smoothly and safely along the way.

If, as we walk, there are too many obstacles or detours, we question whether we're going in the right direction. And anytime that we see someone else stumbling to find his or her way, moving in ways that don't seem as straightforward and logical, we assume that the poor, zigzagging soul has no idea what he or she is doing and is headed down the wrong path.

Isn't that how we secretly look at our friend who has had multiple jobs in different industries? Or who is constantly trying things and failing? The one who every year has a new lifestyle or philosophy, or who got divorced and decided to move three thousand miles away and start an entirely new life? Don't we secretly judge a little bit and think to ourselves, *That person clearly doesn't have it together*. Or maybe that's even how we judge ourselves a little, deep down inside? A little part of us judges the messy journey—others' and our own—because we believe that peace and stability lie in finding the *right* path for our lives.

In Disney's *Moana*, the young heroine sets sail on the rough, open sea to try to save her people. She has never been this far outside of her reef and needs to cross it in order to fulfill her mission. Not knowing exactly where she's going or exactly how to cross the dangerous ocean to get there, Moana asks for the demigod Maui to teach her how to sail. He tells her that it's not sailing that she needs to learn but the ancient art of wayfinding.

In the end, of course, she completes her mission. Could a Disney movie end any other way? I won't spoil it for those of you who haven't seen it, but suffice it to say that where she ends up is far more amazing than anything she could have ever imagined.

I've come to realize that in life, most of us are Moana. Not 100 percent sure of where we are going or how to get there, but knowing that we need some method of navigating the rough seas in order to end up someplace good. And, it turns out that wayfinding is in fact a thing. It is the ancient Polynesian practice of navigating the open oceans. It involves orienting yourself and navigating without a map; having a general vision of where you want to go, even though you can't yet see it, and then using all of the information you have— where you've been, the weather, your current location—to help get you safely to a destination.

In today's world, when there is no map, no guaranteed future, and no single path there, we are called to be wayfinders. Wise, observant, intuitive beings making quick decisions, observing the landscape, and riding the waves to move forward. So what does wayfinding actually look like in our day-to-day lives as we are presented with choices, big and small, about who we want to be, what we want to do with our time, and how we want to change the world? Well, for the journey to unpack and rewrite the stories that are represented here in this book, wayfinding looks like being patient, flexible, and discerning as you go through your own journey. Be willing to experiment, try new things, make mistakes, and try again.

I've laid out these stories in the way that made the most sense for me. In each chapter, I mention how that particular story played a part in my life transformation. But please know that the stories were not mastered in neat, simple steps. Some took me weeks to process, others months, others a year, some I am even still daily wrestling with to ensure my freedom from the old stories.

Because of that, there is no right order in which to approach these topics. You do not have to master one to master the next. Like most stories in our lives, they are all intertwined. My dear friend Rwandan storyteller Clemantine Wamariya talks often about how stories in the West African oral tradition have no beginning and no ending—they weave from one to the other as dynamically and interconnectedly as the pieces of our lives do. So feel free to start with the issue that is holding you back the most. Jump ahead, flip backwards, read and reread . . . Do whatever you need to do to piece together the stories of your life—of our lives—together. My stories are only powerful when they help you rewrite your own and find *your* way. So let's get to work.

PART II

CHAPTER 4

THE STORY OF FEAR

A strange thing happens when you're presented with—or decide to take—your freedom; when the dust settles and you're staring at an open road of questions and possibilities.

Fear comes to meet you.

At least, that's what happened to me.

I assumed that I would wake up each day now with boundless energy, ready to go discover, do, and be something new. Instead, I was paralyzed. In those early days of my journey after I quit my job, the fear was suffocating. It lay on me like a heavy blanket. I hid under it, a huddle of what-ifs.

What if I had made a mistake? What if I couldn't figure out how to make money? What if I really had no idea what I was doing? What if I couldn't live up to other people's expectations of me—or of the ones I had for myself? What if I ended up needing to ask for my job back? What if I failed? What if all of this was for nothing?

To be honest, had I bothered to take a millisecond to think about it, fear likely would have stopped me from quitting my job in the first place.

The lack of clarity about my future—both near and long-term—meant that I was, for the moment, living in the state that I was most afraid of: unsure. And if all of that wasn't enough, the state of uncertainty didn't just leave me feeling fearful. It also left me feeling *guilty for being afraid*. Why? Because nothing about the way I felt or how I was behaving matched up with the image that I had carefully crafted of myself: bold, confident, fearless. So many people had looked up to me. By the age of twenty-four, I had run a high-profile national political youth organization. I was a woman who spoke regularly in front of thousands of people at conferences and rallies. I stood next to elected officials on Capitol Hill introducing legislation and lobbied for policies and programs that met the needs of young people and other underrepresented constituents. On TV, I would go toe-to-toe with angry conservatives, easily standing up to people who challenged my beliefs about right and wrong. I was quite literally paid to be bold and look absolutely fearless.

But the truth was, even though the work itself was easy for me—I could perform fearlessness with the best of them—I was still afraid of something almost every day. Embarrassment, rejection, not being liked, failure, financial insecurity . . . these hidden weaknesses in turn made me feel deeply ashamed, which then left me even more anxious and afraid of being discovered as a fraud—someone too scared to live a big, bold, beautiful life. It was a vicious cycle that had never been more obvious than now, as I anxiously stared at my laptop (or the ceiling) for hours every day, faced with choices to make about who I wanted to be in the world.

While this was probably the most aware of fear I had been in a long time, it was certainly not the only time that fear had shown itself in my life. In fact, much of what had driven me thus far had been unacknowledged but ever-present fear. Fear of disappointing people, of not representing my family or my culture or my faith well, fear of failing, fear of being broke, fear of being exposed as less than perfect . . .

I remember being a little girl, about four or five, sitting on a bicycle on the sidewalk in front of my grandmother's yard. The bike was pink and white with a wicker basket on the front and training wheels on the back. It was the perfect first bicycle, and my uncle Ronnie was teaching me how to ride. Everything was great—until it wasn't.

My memory of the details is fuzzy—he swears that I rolled over a little uneven pavement and took a tiny tumble as I was going *uphill*. How bad could that have been? But in my mind, I was pushed down a slope and crashed. So let's just say that the exact circumstances of my fall are disputed. There *is* something I do distinctly remember though: crying, being picked back up, and deciding in that moment that I absolutely, 100 percent did not want to do it again. I was finished.

My uncle gave the speech that all good adults give children about not giving up, not being a quitter, how if at first you don't succeed try and try again. Blah, blah, blah. But I had made up in my mind: I would never fall again. I would simply stay off of the bicycle.

But why? Why did I react so strongly to that small fall? And what was it that I was so afraid of?

Well, if you break it down, the things that I was afraid of become pretty obvious: First, I was afraid of the pain. I have never been one with a high tolerance for pain, so the thought of scrapes and blood or, God forbid, a broken bone was a pretty solid deterrent for a prissy ribbons-and-bows girl like me.

But a few bruises alone wouldn't have been enough to have me quit forever.

I was also afraid of how I would look both in the moment and after. I liked being good at things. And if falling would make me look funny or silly—if it meant that I could be judged by those watching—I wanted no part of it.

Looking at it now, I can see that the *fear of falling* was a mixed drink made up of *fear of pain*, *fear of appearing less than perfect*, and *fear of judgment* that became the cocktail of my life. Any of those fears sound familiar to you?

Now fast-forward to my fear about quitting my job and starting my new life. Here I was, over twenty years later, a full-blown adult with those same fears deeply entrenched into my psyche. I could not only still not ride a bike, but I was afraid of doing things that I wouldn't easily excel at, afraid of doing things that weren't sure bets, afraid of everything that might actually help me move forward at this moment in my life. I was perpetually afraid to fall. And the only way to not fall was to not move. I was . . . stuck.

But it's no wonder I harbored these fears.

We live in a culture of fear. My fear made perfect sense when put in the context of the world we live in. And yours does too.

From the moment we are born, we are surrounded by clear indicators that the world is a scary place, warnings that at any moment we might stumble upon the experience that sends us free-falling into a devastating outcome. The realities of our world, our collective experience in it, and the ever-present reminders of just how bad things are would be enough to give anyone pause. Most of our fears—in particular those that I hear echoed most often from my peers—can be categorized into a few overarching worries that color our outlook on the world:

- **The fear of financial insecurity.** If you have a lot of money, you're afraid of losing it. If you have some money, you're afraid of not having enough. If you have a little money, you're afraid of poverty. And if you're poor, you're just afraid. And rightfully so. Many of the social systems and structures that we were told would lead to some level of financial security haven't really been working like the instructions inside the box said they would. College degrees have far less economic value in the current market. Incomes are stagnant, and then there's the high level of debt incurred from that questionably valuable education and the general higher cost of living. Half of millennials spend over the recommended 30 percent of their income on rent. And according to rent.com, one out of five are spending *over half of their* income on it. Social Security is on its last legs, and the financial markets are . . . untrustworthy to say the least. If you need to hear more, just turn on the news or open any issue of *Time* magazine. Somewhere in there, you'll find a statement to the effect of "Gen Y is screwed economically. But they're so creative!"

- **The fear of disaster.** From global warming to police brutality, terrorism to deportation, natural disasters to mass shootings, cancer from sun to cancer from meat, just living in today's world can feel like a scene from *The Hunger Games*. Whether the sociopolitical reality is actually scarier now than before, or if our generation's access to information in the 24/7 news cycle has simply made us more aware of how much our world resembles District 11, is hard to determine. Either way, it's hard to not fear for yourself, your people, your country, and your planet continually.

- **The fear of being alone.** How is it that we live in a world of 7 billion people, and yet it seems as if everyone is alone? And even weirder still is that it feels as if no one is alone but you. From the time we have our first crush in school, we long for partnership, companionship, to be chosen by someone special. And while the desire is different for different genders and orientations and cultures, at some point, if you haven't landed the perfect relationship (however you define that), desperation kicks in. *What happens if I'm alone, if I never find "the one"?*

- **The fear of failure or of not living up to others' expectations.** I felt this one especially as a woman of color. And while this isn't a uniquely generational concern, the fear of not living up to outdated societal norms is more intense now than ever because of the number of unrealistic, competing expectations that exist. Many of the things that we've been taught to fear—divorce, joblessness and career instability, sickness, infertility—are happening all around us at increasing rates, and even though there are real fixes for them, it doesn't make the underlying fear subside.

- **FOMO (the fear of missing out).** This isn't just a cute acronym. The endless number of choices that are presented to us in every area of life—no matter how many are actually within reach or are good for us—can prove to be paralyzing. We swipe right on the Tinder of life—internships, schools, jobs, apartments, partners—always looking for the best option, a better deal. We spend way too much of our day/night trying to be at the right place at the right time so as not to miss out on anything that could have been somehow . . . "righter." The "rightest," even. The fear of missing out, and of being less than perfect, having something less than what we assume other people's lives are like, causes many of us not just to feel bad and shameful, but to make decisions that may not be the best for our individual selves.

It's no wonder that millennials are the most anxious generation in history. Jean Twenge, a social psychologist at San Diego State University, has studied the underlying story of this generation's fear and anxiety, and sums it up like this: "The research tells us that modern life is not good for mental health."

Sometimes, these fears are strengthened by firsthand experiences— the stories that we have seen with our own eyes that taught us powerful lessons about how the world works. Anything that we have witnessed or experienced can heavily contribute to the cultural narrative of fear.

Your fear of financial insecurity may have come from seeing a parent struggle to make ends meet. Or if you know someone who lost a job and ended up losing his or her house. Or if you saw half of your friends graduate into jobs where they were wildly overqualified and underpaid. Here's the worst part: The existence of all of these reasons to fear provides the perfect vulnerabilities for consumer culture to prey on. It behooves media, business, political, and even religious institutions to remind us of all there is to fear. That way we turn to them for safety and protection (or whatever they are selling that will supposedly save us from the exact thing we are afraid of). In fact, *many of our desires are attempts to avoid our worst fears.*

QUESTION 1: What is the story?

So, after the world has painstakingly reinforced many reasons to fear, what story have we been taught as a response? What is the message that we have been told as a way to combat the fear?

Be fearless.

We are expected to see and know and even run away from all there is to fear without somehow being afraid ourselves. From an early age, insults shame the fearful. We hear taunts of "scaredy cat" on the playground and grow up with the labels "punk" or "pussy" (which makes no sense when one actually realizes the strength and power of the vagina, but I digress). Over and over again, we hear the story that to be afraid is to be weak or childish, and that one of the ultimate signs of maturity is to be unafraid.

Fearlessness as a goal is even entrenched in our spiritual traditions. In Christianity, we are taught to fear nothing other than God. From the story of David and Goliath to Jesus's instructing Peter to "Be not afraid" while he was literally walking on water, we learn that *fear is the opposite of faith.* Scripture not only states that God did not give us a spirit of fear, but it teaches us that to fear is to doubt God. Who wants to do that?

Hindus' sacred text, the Bhagavad Gita, teaches that fearlessness is the first requisite of spirituality, and in Buddhism, the path to enlightenment involves first eliminating all fear. As a lover of religion, I can have respect for these ideas while also recognizing that they are often taken out of context—as most things are in our sound-bite culture—as nothing more than incomplete thoughts that lift up fearlessness as the highest goal.

The cultural story of fearlessness is even louder if you are a man. Guys are supposed to be the slayers of dragons, the poker players with ice in their veins, the protectors, the gangstas, the lone cowboys, the ones who jump in front of speeding bullets to protect the damsels in distress.

But don't worry—men don't get all the fearless fun. There is, of course, the trope of the "strong black woman." We are supposed to charge into life's fires, without pause, to fix, save, or carry on our backs whatever needs to be fixed, saved, or carried. As black women, we are often depicted as the ones who can handle *anything*. Even the late legendary feminist Audre Lorde (patron saint of black girl magic) said so, right? She is the source of a line that I was once *this* close to getting tattooed in huge letters across my back: "I am deliberate and afraid of nothing."

When I hear it, I picture her, clear-eyed, steely, and calm with her Afro popping and her armor on, deliberately and fearlessly facing down the demons of sexism and racism, like a womanist superhero, a goddess, impervious to life's terrors.

For years, I made her quote my mantra, repeating it over and over again with the hope that one day it would become true for me. Perhaps one day I too could be afraid of nothing. But somehow, new fears kept popping up in my life, like that game of Whac-A-Mole at

Chuck E. Cheese. The mantra just wasn't enough. Why couldn't I be as fearless as Audre?

Perhaps because if any of us ever bothered to look for the *context* of that popular quote, we would see that it comes at the end of her poem "New Year's Day." Not a speech. Not a conversation. Not an interview. But a poem. Poetry is often used to describe our desires, not our realities. In this poem, Audre was describing a specific day, a day when the rain fell like tar on her skin and for some reason, in that very moment, she felt no fear. One single day. Perhaps even one that she longed for in real life and hadn't yet experienced. Perhaps she was simply fantasizing about this perfect moment in which all of her fear would disappear. In either case, real or imagined, she was describing a specific time, not a constant state of being.

Knowing this, I no longer see her as this steely, fearless superhero but instead as a human mother, sitting at the end of a long day, letting tears fall, as she says, not "from sadness but from grit," and acknowledging that right now, on this night and in this world of very scary things, she was ready to let it all go and be afraid of nothing. I wonder if she felt just as unafraid the next morning.

And I wonder how she would respond if she knew that her line about one single day had been used to create an unattainable lifetime ideal for a generation of women?

QUESTION 2: Does this story serve my values and me?

I came to realize the ultimate problem with the ideal of fearlessness: *Fear is natural.* It is a primitive, instinctive, evolutionarily biological (and often logical) reaction to the threat of pain of any kind, real or perceived. Walking through life with a mandate to eliminate it denies humanity, ignores realities, and ultimately leaves many of us tangled up in a web of guilt and shame.

It was clear that for me, the "have no fear" mantra hadn't been effective in the face of my current realities. All it had done was bring more judgment, anxiety, and pressure to eliminate the fear that was constantly arising.

Having fears didn't mean that I was weak or ill-equipped to succeed at life. It just meant that I was as human as anyone else. The truth is that no matter how fierce, smart, and confident we are, no matter how many difficult things we are able to face and overcome, or how many risks we choose to take, we are human. To quote *Grey's Anatomy* star and activist Jesse Williams, "Just because we are magic doesn't mean that we aren't real." And as real people in a very real world, it is okay for us to feel afraid.

This encouragement that I gave myself and am giving you now is completely at odds with most self-help literature, so I want you to take a minute and pause. The gurus say that the way to conquer our fears is to recognize that they are imaginary.

To that end, I once saw an acronym that spelled out "fear" with the words False Evidence Appearing Real. Like most motivational pop psychology, it sounded great. We have nothing to fear but fear itself, right? In this thinking, the things that we fear are simply mirages, boogeymen that haunt us at night but will disappear in the light of day.

But how could this be?

The row of abandoned, foreclosed homes with people's furniture on the front lawn in my neighborhood in 2008 wasn't false. *It was real.*

My female colleague getting fired, insulted by the police, and humiliated in court, all for reporting an incident of sexual harassment, actually happened.

The videos of young black people being harassed, arrested, shot, and killed by police that play on repeat every day on the news aren't fake.

My thirty-seven-year-old friend who is unable to get pregnant and is now spending tens of thousands of dollars on
fertility treatments, while still being told that it's "too late" by
her doctors, is real.

Without context, False Evidence Appearing Real is dangerously
misleading and perhaps even a bit insulting. To deny the existence of
fear is to ignore our reality.

I needed a story about fear that was honest, that didn't cause me
to deny it for the sake of some Girl Scout "fearlessness" badge.

But how could I have that without also being overwhelmed by
the fear? Living in fear certainly wouldn't match my values either.
I didn't believe in being held hostage to anything, no matter how
real. And when I unpacked each fear, it became clear that underneath
them all were deeper worries that were grounded in dangerous stories and values that were antithetical to my own. Here's what I mean.

Sure, the fear of not being able to afford a house—or worse yet,
of having one and then losing it—is real. But underneath that lies the
belief that without a house I am somehow inferior, a failure of the
American Dream. We believe that the humiliation and the failure
will destroy us. And that just isn't true.

Sure, the fear of infertility is real. But the belief underneath the
fear is that not being able to birth a biological child somehow makes
me less of a woman. That idea is false and does not match up with
my beliefs that as a woman, I am more than my body or the roles that
society has taught me to play.

See what I mean?

The fear of undesired outcomes makes total sense, but what those
outcomes will truly mean for your identity and your life may not.

Fear as a natural instinct may help us *survive*, but allowing it to
take root, reinforce untrue beliefs, and dictate our lives can absolutely
keep us from *thriving*. Like an anchor, it can keep you safe in a storm

but stuck when it's time to move. Allowing fear to prevent me from making necessary changes in my life would mean that I was letting fear take away my freedom. I couldn't live in fear and be who I wanted to be.

QUESTION 3: What if I believed something else?

Ultimately, this dance with fear had to happen on a tightrope, not tipping too much one way or the other. And I needed—we all need—a story that helped me find the balance and truth that my life deserves. I needed a story about fear that would acknowledge the context and circumstances of my life and who I was without paralyzing and disempowering me.

So I asked myself these questions: *What if I stopped worrying about being fearless and instead worked toward learning how to move confidently with fear in tow? What if I began to accept the reality of fear, but instead of letting it weigh me down or cause me to feel ashamed and paralyzed, I refocused my energy to push past it?* In short, *What if I was brave?*

If fearlessness is the absence of fear, bravery is the determination to do something despite its continued presence. It is a way of looking at scary realities and conditions, acknowledging the presence of fear, and then making the choice to do what needs to be done anyway. Bravery does not waste time feeling angry at the fear or ashamed of it being there in the first place. Bravery doesn't taunt you like a school bully, mocking your anxiety or worry. And bravery doesn't tell you to ignore risk and live life like a daredevil. It simply says, "Yep. This is scary. Now, what do we do about it?"

In this story, faith isn't the absence of fear. It is trust and hope *through* the fear.

We have to be brave enough to face the fear of falling—the pain, the judgment—with what we know to be true: our inherent worth, our resilience, our ability to survive no matter what.

Fears that don't take those true things into account are the fears that *aren't real*. And the ones that we have to be brave enough to face.

Bravery means that we are willing to feel the fear and do something anyway—because what we are moving toward is better than this, better than fear could ever be.

QUESTION 4: What can this new story look like for me?

In order to move forward and take the leaps that were necessary for my new life, I needed to figure out what bravery actually looked like. There were still so many things to consider: How would bravery impact my decision making? What about risk? What if . . . I actually fell? How did one actually *do* it?

Outside of low-budget horror films where main characters stupidly walk *toward* the murderer, I had never really stopped to witness what it looks like when a real person exhibits bravery.

Enter my friend, Jose Antonio Vargas. By his mid-twenties, Jose was a Pulitzer Prize–winning Filipino American journalist who by all indications was winning at life. But Jose had a secret. Even though Jose had been raised in America, when he was sixteen he asked his grandfather for his Social Security number so that he could get his driver's license. He discovered then that unbeknownst to him, he was not actually an American citizen. He had been brought to the U.S. by his family as a child, to have a better life, and now, after building that better life, he was among the estimated 11.3 million undocumented immigrants that Pew has calculated live in this country, the ones that are talked about all day long on cable news.

Jose held on to that secret for years, hoping that no one would know. He went to college and built a successful career as a journalist. But in 2011, as the political debate on immigration heated up, with old white men in Congress deciding who was and was not an American, and old white men in coffee shops cursing at young brown "illegals," something inside of him broke. He couldn't stay silent any longer. He was tired of living "in the closet," watching those just like him fighting a fight for their livelihoods. He decided that it was time to come out and tell the world of his immigration status.

The risks were *tremendous*. He spoke to former colleagues, his relatives, friends, and lawyers, to get advice and also warn them of what he was about to do. He wanted to make sure that his actions didn't harm anyone else in the process. And once he had done all he could to prepare those close to him, he did the bravest thing: In June 2011, Jose published a groundbreaking essay in the *New York Times Magazine* in which he revealed and chronicled his life in America as an undocumented immigrant. That one choice changed the trajectory of his life forever. Overnight, he became a new face of the immigrant rights movement. Everyone wanted to talk to him about his experience—elected officials, media, and other young immigrants. As the policy debate in Washington reached a fever pitch, Jose appeared on the cover of *Time* magazine.

Today, Jose is one of this country's most recognizable immigration rights activists. He runs a nonprofit organization and media company called Define American that uses storytelling to humanize the conversation around immigration and identity. But even with that success, he talks frequently and openly about how he still lives in fear every day. He is constantly afraid, not only of deportation, but also of violence from those who don't believe that he is an American. Yet he persists, trying his hardest to get his citizenship and using his voice to encourage people to come out of the shadows in the only country they have ever known, the country that they contribute to and love.

To me, that's what real bravery looks like.

YOUR TURN

Sure, some of us might feel compelled or called like Jose to push past fear and do the groundbreaking public work that could cost us everything. But more often than not, the fears that paralyze us are the ones that risk our most private possessions: more everyday things, like our ego, our comfort, our security, our emotions.

- Where are the opportunities to be brave in a world that looks like it is on the verge of collapse every day?

- What might it look like to be brave in the face of an unstable economy?

- How can you be brave and not desperate in your relationship with your desire for companionship?

- Is it possible to be brave and honest about your reality in the face of a world putting forth a Photoshopped, social media–ready facade?

- How can you bravely face all of the options that your daily life provides you, stare FOMO in the face, and be satisfied with a choice?

Only you can answer these questions for yourself, but I'll share the process that can help you begin. See, bravery isn't just about recklessly leaping with no thought for the consequences.

In Jose's story:

1. He *felt a calling* to do something. To tell his story.

2. He *acknowledged and felt the fear*.

3. He *assessed the cost* by thinking about what he could lose and what he would gain. He spoke to his mentors, his family, and his friends. He weighed his career against his values.

4. He did whatever he could to *mitigate risk*. He warned his boss, family, and friends and got a good lawyer.

5. And then he *did it*.

Taking these five steps in the process of being brave is a guided way to manage and respond to the fear that grips you and threatens to hold you back.

Jose didn't then—nor does he years later—know how the story will end. Nor will you. Bravery does not guarantee a positive outcome. But I am finding out that something freer, more beautiful, more aligned with your calling, lies on the other side of the mountains that you are afraid to climb, even if you fall on the way up.

PRACTICE, PRACTICE, PRACTICE

Just as narrative intelligence requires practice, so does bravery. I decided to proactively put myself in low-risk situations to exercise the bravery muscle and teach myself my new story.

In the weeks and months ahead, I did everything from going to networking events by myself (my worst social nightmare) to cutting my long, thick hair and shaving one side (hated it). I even took a trapeze class just for the "fun" of it. Those actions prepared me for the inevitable choices that I would have to make in choosing a new career, in admitting my confusion to the world, in examining my environment, and in reinventing myself and my beliefs.

The trapeze class episode in particular taught me a lesson that puts it all in perspective. As you can imagine, when it came time to climb up to the trapeze, I was, to put it lightly, afraid. The old me would have spent thirty minutes on the ground, going back and forth between utter terror (the story of fear) and then trying to convince myself that there was nothing to be afraid of at all (the story of fearlessness), ultimately leaving the gym in complete failure.

Instead, I said to myself, *Look, is there some risk? Yes. But you assessed it before even showing up and decided that this experience was worth more than the slight risk. You have done everything you can to mitigate risk—you have gone through the three-hour training, you have practiced, you have tightened your harness. So now, let's be brave.*

As I climbed the ladder, my heart felt like it was going to beat out of my chest. When I got up there, I counted to ten, opened my mouth wide, and jumped, allowing a bloodcurdling scream to erupt that lasted *the entire time I was in the air.*

When it came time to climb again, I just knew that the second time would be better. But sure enough, as I got on the ladder, my heart started pounding again, just as loudly as before. And once again, when it was time to jump, I compulsively opened my mouth to let out a scream that sounded like I was being murdered. It was even more embarrassing the second time around because clearly, my brain knew that I could do this. I did it three more times in the class, each time having the same reaction, undoubtedly looking to the small bodies below like a complete nut job. It turns out, my version of jumping will always look more like sliding, screaming, and flailing off the edge.

As I began the process of rewiring my life, I made a promise to myself: I would be brave. No matter what changes or choices I would need to make, I would throw my head back, scream, and fly. I was ready to jump, to move, and to run toward my new destiny.

While sometimes being brave and doing the scary thing will eliminate your fear forever, sometimes it won't. You may always be afraid of failure, of being unliked, of making a terrible mistake, or of an evil reality TV star winning the presidency and leading us to World War III. Those stories may never fully disappear.

Just make sure that when it's time to fly, you fly.

OLD STORY: Be fearless.

TRUE STORY: Be brave in the face of fear.

CHAPTER 5

THE STORY OF DREAMS

S o . . . uhhh . . . what exactly do you want to do?

I heard the tone in my sweet new husband's voice as he asked me that question one day, weeks into my "new life." He had watched me spend my days updating my website, playing with consulting company titles, designing business cards, and crying. A few days after my epic mic drop I received a call out of the blue asking if I was interested in doing some freelance work for a major company—a request that felt like manna from heaven seeing as how I had never done corporate consulting, let alone at this scale. I took it as a sign that I was moving in the right direction and that I would at least have a few dollars coming in for the next few months. But that was just one project, and it wasn't moving me any closer to a new life. I was still aimless and confused, each day babbling vague language about "starting over" and "living my best life."

Finally, Lifetime Bae asked me the question that any sane person would. There was no tone of frustration when he said it. In fact, he asked it tentatively, delicately, as if he were handling an explosive device. He knew that was the million-dollar question. It was the question that I had already spent a good chunk of time asking myself. "What exactly do you want?"

If all the *shoulds* were stripped away, if I dared to imagine that I could create a new life, the circumstances would suddenly beg the question: What kind of life did I actually want to live?

Ultimately, that's what all of this was about. Figuring out the contours, shapes, and colors of a life that fit me better than my old one.

I thought for a minute as my husband stared at me, kindly waiting for an answer. After a long pause, I spit out the only words that came to mind: "I want to live the life of my dreams."

I was immediately embarrassed. I had answered that question like a child or a Hollywood actress. The life of my dreams? What did that even mean? Why did I say that?

But, in some ways, it made sense. Ever since I could remember, all of my ideas about the future had been dripping with the language of dreams.

I had been the little girl with big dreams. I'd heard enough tragic stories about adults who had never followed their dreams; men and women in their forties and fifties who had let the weight of the world squash their hopes and thwart their pursuit of the life they had fantasized about when they were younger. That would not happen to me. I believed wholeheartedly that dreaming big, audacious dreams and following them until they came true was a surefire method to achieve fulfillment. My dreams would be the ultimate markers of success: If ... when ... I achieved them, I would then be able to stand at the finish line of life and claim victory.

Yet somehow, as the realities of adulthood had crept in, no matter how much time I spent talking or thinking about my dreams, I often found myself making choices that were practical and smart, driven more by immediate needs and realism than by fantasies and desires. Perhaps this was the culprit of my discontent?

Now, in this moment of re-creation, perhaps I should dust myself off, reapply myself, and get back to the business of dreaming big.

The problem was, I wasn't entirely sure what that meant.

What did the life of my dreams really look like? What would it feel like, smell like, taste like? And how would I know when I had it?

And so it seemed to me that if living the life of my dreams was the goal—one that felt perfectly aligned with my newfound boldness and freedom—I needed to familiarize myself with those dreams.

Opening my journal at that time, one would have found lists and lists of desired achievements and material possessions: Winning high honors like an Emmy or a MacArthur Genius Grant. Delivering a TED Talk. I wanted to be rich enough to buy myself a mansion and buy my mother her dream home. I had dreams of having a property that was big enough to double as a home away from home for my big extended family. I had dreams of writing multiple bestselling books. Of building a media empire. Of jet-setting all over the world with LB, having my two perfect brown children with me at all times. And all of those dreams corresponded to perfectly cut-out pictures on the vision boards hanging in my closet. Pictures of vacation homes and master bedrooms, luxury cars and this one random photo of a pregnant Amber Rose in a prenatal yoga class—because of course, in the midst of running an empire, traveling the world, and raising a family, I would also have time for perfectly done nails and yoga.

There were a lot of dreams there, but as I looked at them all, one recurring theme emerged. Somehow no matter which aspect of my dream life I was fantasizing about, Oprah was somewhere in the mix. In fact, Mama O had somehow managed to appear on my vision board six different times. Pictures of her interviewing, pictures of her on TV, pictures of her book club, pictures of her in her perfect garden with her perfect vegetables and perfect hair.

So yes. When I asked myself what a life of my dreams looked like, a little voice inside whispered: *Oprah.*

How cliché. *You are an intellectual,* I said to myself. *You are an artist. You are an* activist, *for God's sake. And the best you can come up with for what a life of your dreams looks like is being Oprah?*

Hell yes. Becoming Oprah's protégée and successor, to be exact.

And while that may sound ridiculous to some of you, any black girl who is talkative and was a child of the nineties has at some point either thought about or been told that she reminds some well-meaning adult of Oprah. It's like how from 2008 on, every intelligent black boy will hear that he could be the next Obama. These are just the cultural references that people have and things that people say. But I took those words to heart.

When I was a little girl, I would sit in my room with my friends (or more often than not, by myself) and make believe that I was on *The Oprah Winfrey Show.* Usually, I would play both parts, her and the guest. I could do this for hours, innocent, carefree, joyous. To me, it wasn't just make-believe; it was practice. I knew that I had at least twenty or thirty years ahead of me to make this dream a reality.

As I got older, the dream got more specific. Oprah would hear of my "work" (the work itself was never specific in this imagined scenario, though, just some vague sense of demonstrating my greatness in the world). She would insist on meeting me. I would go on her show, and we would hit it off right away. I would impress her with my insights, my communication skills, and my overall joie de vivre. She would tell me that it was *one of the best conversations she'd ever had* and that she saw a little of herself in me, whether from our church roots or our brief experience in pageants or our love of reading. And from there, a lifelong relationship would develop. She would have me on her show several more times, becoming an auntie/mentor/fairy godmother of sorts. Her audience would love me, and then, one day, out of the blue, she would offer me my own show, passing the mantle on from her to me. The end.

This dream brought me much joy as a little girl. But as an adult, it had become a source of embarrassment, disappointment, and—dare I say it—pain. As each year went by and my life seemed nothing like the life I fantasized about and I was no closer to hanging out with Oprah in her Santa Barbara garden, I was constantly aware of the voice in my head telling me that I had made all the wrong decisions. That following my heart and changing my major from journalism to African American studies was the dumbest thing I could have ever done. That being swept away by my desire to change the world and work in civil and human rights had set me back irrevocably. That the work that I was doing would never lead me to that dream. The voice in my head taunted me, asking how stupid was I to think that with all of the talented, ambitious women in the world—many of whom were actively pitching TV shows and hosting already—somehow I could become the next Oprah?

But now, with no job and no real plan, maybe it was the perfect time to recommit myself to this endeavor. According to all of the messages and stories around me, there was never a wrong time to follow my dreams, right? That's what I should have been doing all along, right? RIGHT?

QUESTION 1: What is the story?

It's hard to pinpoint the exact origin of the "follow your dreams" story, as dreams are a vital component of spiritual practices all around the world and have been since ancient times. But America has a very specific way of separating them from any spiritual context and making them solely about accomplishment, achievement, acquisition, and ambition. This secular framing makes sense when you think about the foundation of the American Experiment itself. In his *Time* magazine piece "The American Dream: A Biography," writer Jon Meacham wrote, "Dreams of God and gold made America possible." The settlers were running from religious persecution and seeking a place with untapped riches and wealth as their refuge. In essence, our country was built on dreams. Sure, those dreams also involved wholesale theft of land, the massacre of a people, and slavery, but yes, it was all in pursuit of a dream.

So the "follow your dreams" story is taught to us from an early age. Some of us hear it from loving, supportive parents. Others may hear it from encouraging, well-meaning teachers or other adults telling us that the sky is the limit and that "if you dream it, you can achieve it." And even if you didn't get that kind of direct, personal encouragement—not everyone grew up in supportive, nurturing environments—you certainly heard it from the greatest life coach of all: popular culture. It's the number one piece of advice given by celebrities, the kind of simple story that makes us feel good and believe that dreaming big dreams and doggedly pursuing them is all that success and happiness require.

I can still hear the melody to Disney's *Cinderella* in my head:

> *Have faith in your dreams and someday*
> *Your rainbow will come smiling through*

Or what about the iconic opening line of Notorious B.I.G.'s "Juicy" ... "It was all a dream!" B.I.G. goes on to express joy at having realized his childhood dream of being a rapper. In his new life, he could see the dream that he had achieved in his possessions: condos, diamonds, cars, women, and enough money to take care of those he loved.

Hip-hop often gets erroneously blamed for introducing materialism to the mainstream, but the reality is, in America, dreams have long been just as much about a lifestyle as about accomplishment. Our dreams aren't just supposed to be about who we want to be. They are often about what we want to have and what we want our life to look like when we become that person. In America, we *are* our dreams, and in many cases, depending on our background, they are all we have. As the "Juicy" chorus says,

You know very well, who you are,
don't let them hold you down, reach for the stars.

In Indian-American comedian Hasan Minhaj's hilariously poignant Netflix special, *Homecoming King*, he recalls the first time he visited one of his white friends at her house after school. Sitting at their dinner table, her parents asked him a question that he'd never heard before: "Hasan, what are you *into*?" In the special, Hasan plays that scene for laughs, highlighting how in his immigrant household, he'd never been asked about his passions or what he wanted to be when he grew up. After he thinks for a minute and comes up with a random answer ("maybe acoustic guitar?"), the white parents smile and sweetly tell him to "follow his dreams." Upon hearing those words, Hasan opens his eyes wide as if he's seen the light. He looks off into the distance, cocks his head, pondering this new idea, and says, "You know what? I think I will!" That was the moment when he was introduced to the American idea that our dreams—the things that we want in life—are not only okay, but should determine what we pursue and how we live.

The basic premise of the American Dream is that "the dream," whether it be independence or material prosperity, is equally accessible to anyone. (Regardless of how untrue that has been and continues to be for large swaths of the population.) The idea was baked right into the Declaration of Independence: The pursuit of happiness is a noble one. What could make us happier than achieving our wildest dreams?

If you think about it, this was the nation's first strategic marketing campaign: Let's build a society upon the notion of the *accessibility of dreams*, and we'll attract lots of folks who are looking for a better life. I can see the brochure now . . .

And the marketing worked. We have been taught that the American legacy of achievement and innovation starts with the prototype of the intrepid dreamer. From Walt Disney—a man who darn near got high off of the idea of dreams—to modern-day icons like Steve Jobs and, my personal favorite, Diddy, dreams are manna from heaven that are 100 percent attainable with dogged pursuit. In this story, it is our dreams that lead us to new life.

Whether there are aspects of the American Dream story that you find helpful or not, it is clear that to believe this narrative as gospel means that you have taken what began as a great marketing strategy and turned it into a life philosophy.

Just how far has this idea gone? Well, look no further than the bestselling book *The Secret*. It exploded on the scene over a decade ago, and to borrow a line from Drake, after that, "nothing was the same." An updated version of its predecessor, *The Law of Attraction*, *The Secret* spawned an entire cottage industry of books, conferences, motivational speakers, and YouTube experts who all believe in and teach "the art of manifesting."

The premise of manifesting is that if you focus on your desires long and hard enough, eliminating all the negative energy that might block them, they absolutely, without a doubt, 100 percent will come true. In this school of thought, following your dreams *is a real, metaphysical law.* The imprint of that story is visible everywhere, from coffee mugs to televangelism to Instagram. Just Google "celebrities and the law of attraction."

Unfortunately, not much of the American culture of having and following big dreams explores the merit of the dreams themselves— whether or not they are right for you and whether or not a single-minded focus on them will actually yield a fulfilling life. By not questioning dreams and issuing a blanket mandate about the importance of following them, the broader cultural story brushes over an important truth: that most dreams that you have actually came from somewhere else, something outside of you. What you *think* you want, what you *think* you desire, is largely shaped by the stories you've consumed about what a desirable life looks like. Your dreams are shaped by external narratives around success, money, accomplishment, love, and the like. That doesn't make them wrong, but it also doesn't make them right.

And as cultures change, so do their dreams. In a culture that equates size with power, we dream of big things. In a society that treats wealth as a virtue, our dreams involve material wealth. In a society where ownership is prized, our dreams are about homes and land. In a society where fame is a drug, we dream of celebrity as success. And because the American idea of dreams is so disconnected from spirituality, many of the dreams that we hold up as guides are interpreted as organic goals that erupted from somewhere deep inside of us.

We Are a Generation of Dreamers

This message is pushed down our throats at every turn. In every commencement speech from kindergarten to college, we are told to chase our dreams, keep them in sight, and never let them die. We wonder, like Langston Hughes, about what happens to a dream deferred, and in order to avoid discovering the answer, those of us with ambition use our dreams as the guiding force in our lives. We are, of course, not the first generation to have dreams, but we *are* a generation in which the idea has become both central and essential. Thanks to ever-present voices of motivation and inspiration in our worlds—online and off—we rap about dreams, tattoo quotes about them on our rib cages, and glue three dozen pictures of them to vision boards. They are the answer when life gets hard, and the thing we hold on to for hope, even in the face of a stark reality.

We're not supposed to have just *any* dreams: We're supposed to always shoot for the big ones. We've been taught that dreaming big is *the key* to success, that the answer to figuring out what we should be striving to achieve can be found in these mythical, magical dreams, and that if we visualize and fixate on them long and hard enough, they will guide us in the right direction and, ultimately, come true.

Thanks to my newfound commitment to examine every story, looking at the walls in my crooked room and questioning them—in this case, my own personal dreams of success, wealth, and Oprahdom—I had to admit that my relationship to these fantasies had become a bit more complicated. I still held on tight to them, still posted memes about them, but deep down, I had started to wonder if my obsession with them was . . . well . . . *helpful.*

Fantasizing about a specific job, a specific house, a specific dollar amount in my bank account, specific vacations, specific accolades, and specific experiences had started to feel not only cliché but, ironically, a bit limiting. Sure they were big, but by believing in them so much, by using them as the single focus of all my hope, was I leaving room for any other possible future? And if I started to question them, did that just make me cynical? Was it a defeatist mind-set? Or was my doubt just proof that I didn't believe in myself enough to make my dreams come true? These are the questions you're not supposed to pose in public, lest you sound small-minded and uninspired, but the truth is, I'd started to question my dreams and the role they played in my life.

If I was going to orient my new life around following and actual-izing my wildest dreams, whatever they might be, I needed to make sure that my dreams were actually serving me. I needed to soberly evaluate whether or not the pursuit of my dreams was the best use of my time and energy.

Was this big story about following my dreams actually serving me?

QUESTION 2: Does this story serve my values and me?

I decided to take my Oprah dream for a spin. How did it make me feel? Where did it come from? Why had I held on to it for so long?

Dreams are never as simple as they seem. Beneath each one is a story, pulled from stories that the world has taught us about what we need to be happy and successful.

And so, I wondered, what was the story underneath my Oprah dream that had shaped it in the first place? Why did I want *this* thing so badly?

To answer, I had to do some serious soul-searching. After asking, *Why this dream? Why is this what I want? Why does this matter?* and responding to each answer with every toddler's favorite word—*Why?*—again and again, what I found, after some radical honestly, was pretty surprising.

It turns out, there were two major reasons that I was drawn to this particular dream. And neither was really about Oprah at all.

The first was a pretty uncomfortable truth. My dream had a lot to do with my *desire to be chosen*. My obsession wasn't so much with her as it was with the idea of a powerful, rich, well-loved woman thinking that I was special enough to hand me the keys to her kingdom. Connecting with Oprah represented validation, approval, and, if I'm honest, a lottery-winner story that would allow me to bypass the hard, risky work of trying to build my own kingdom myself.

How . . . pathetic. On the surface, there was nothing wrong with seeking recognition from one of the most successful women in media, right? But underneath was a story that exposed my own insecurities and neediness. Talk about a reality check.

And the checks—the reality kind, not the money kind—kept coming. I don't know if you're a believer in signs, but I am. Over the course of my journey year, the signs that my Oprah dream may not be the right fit for me kept revealing themselves. As the ancient stoic philosopher Seneca once said, sometimes the "things we hope for mock us."

I was given tickets to attend a *Fast Company* conference. I registered online and received all the materials telling me how to sign up for sessions and an off-site "field trip." But when I went to log in, the website was down. I emailed the conference administrator and was told that they had heard about technical difficulties and not to worry; I could see my options and sign up at the event. When the day came,

I arrived at the conference and was immediately surrounded by a group of thirty to forty beaming, excited people, all coming through the door at the same time. They were out of breath, passing around their phones, and talking about "how amazing it was." Giddy is the only word I can use to describe them. I asked a stranger what the hoopla was about, and she replied with a sense of breathless joy, "We signed up to go on the private tour of OWN's offices, and Oprah herself came through and hung out with us. We talked to her, took pictures, and it was great."

Excuse me? I had missed meeting Oprah and becoming her BFF simply because of a technical difficulty?

You know what? I said to myself. *Perhaps this is just an example of God making me really work to achieve this dream.* Everything happens for a reason, right? I still wasn't getting the message.

One day, months later, Oprah and her team decided to identify one hundred people who were changing the world and call this group her Super Soul 100. On that list of one hundred extraordinary people, I *personally knew twenty*. WTF. How in the world could twenty people around me have been hand-selected by Oprah? Sure, I could focus on the blessing of calling that many beautiful, brilliant people friends. But also . . . really? Really?

And if that wasn't enough, then came the final sign. It was like God stepping in and saying, "Okay, girl. It's time to wrap this dream up."

One day, while backstage at a conference, in the speakers' lounge, I met a woman who was in senior management at OWN. She was just a few years older than me, African American, and fierce. We hit it off instantly (or so I thought) and talked, having been assured by our mutual friend, organizer of said conference, that we were destined to be best friends and work together somehow. *This is my shot*, I thought. I shared ideas that I'd had for how OWN could reach more millennial women, the kind of expert voices that I'd love to see on the network, how they could be responding to the current political climate while still remaining on brand. I'm telling you, I pulled out my best stuff. My new best friend asked me about my career and said that we were "kindred spirits." And when it was over, she agreed that we should get together for lunch. I walked right over to LB, who had been standing at the door ready to go for a half hour, and proudly said these exact words, "My dream is about to come true."

Well, it didn't.

After several unanswered email follow-ups, unconfirmed appointments, and last-minute cancellations, it became clear to me that this woman was not all that interested in talking to me. I usually have a firm rule—never email a person back more than twice, for my sake and for theirs. Well, I broke this rule and then some. In any other situation, I would have simply called that being thirsty. But here, I had convinced myself that my embarrassing pursuit of this woman in the face of her obvious disinterest was just a sign of my commitment and determination. You know, following my dreams.

Finally, one day, after coming back home from actually being stood up for a lunch appointment with her that I had scheduled and never really received a confirmation for, LB decided to hand me back a shred of my dignity. Holding my hand, he softly said, "Boo, you're gonna have to let it go." He was right.

Chasing this big dream had not led me to a good place. It had become an obsession that didn't leave me feeling motivated or empowered. It just left me feeling disappointed, desperate, and dis-tracted from the valuable work I could be putting my energy toward. In that moment, I had to remind myself of my values: I was not put on this earth to chase after another human. I was not put on this earth to seek validation. And blindly following a dream that depended on that strategy wasn't such a good idea.

QUESTION 3: What if I believed something else?

Sometimes, no matter how empowering or harmless our dreams sound, all they are is a response to our insecurities or to values that conflict with who we really are.

We dream of more because we feel less than.

We dream of big because we feel small.

We dream of the other side because we know it must be greener than where we are and where we've come from.

It's no coincidence that we call our hopes for our future the same thing that we call the stories that we see in our mind while we are sleeping. But how helpful are they when we're awake?

The Oprah dream hadn't led me to the ideal outcome. That was painfully obvious. But at the very least shouldn't it have been bringing me motivation and inspiration? Aim for the moon, land in the stars, right? In other words, if following dreams is a worthwhile story, the mere pursuit should be helpful, regardless of the outcome. But is that true?

Remember how I said that when I asked myself *why this dream*, I uncovered *two* major reasons? The first was a story about validation, and I finally had to acknowledge that desperation wasn't a great color on me. But the second reason wasn't actually bad. There was a reason that I chose Oprah and not, say, Whitney Houston or Bill Gates or a doctor or a politician. Hidden within this dream were clues about what kind of work I was drawn to in the world. I didn't pick just any successful person. I picked a woman who had built a career using her authentic voice and her gift of gab to share stories and important messages that help people. Isn't that what I *really* wanted to do?

In some ways, that underlying affinity pointed me toward my purpose. Now, I know *purpose* is an overused buzzword. In fact, it's one of those vaguely spiritual concepts that often doesn't have a clear definition. The best one I ever found was inspired by "America's Bishop" T.

D. Jakes. To illustrate what purpose is, Jakes described being on stage and walking over to sit on top of a huge floor speaker, the kind that looks like a big black boom box. "I was sitting on a speaker and I said, 'This speaker will bear the weight of my body. It will make a chair in a pinch.' But it was not designed to be a chair. I am not using it for its highest and best use. Many times we are pushed into functioning in an area that is not our highest and best use because someone needed us to be something we were not created to be."

Purpose is simply your highest and best use. I had spent a lot of time thinking about how my skills and talents could be best used. What I wanted my life to be about and why. And while I wasn't sure exactly what specific job or career was right for me, I felt like I had a good sense of the underlying mission.

I wanted to use my voice to share ideas and messages that helped people survive, thrive, and change the world. (No, I didn't have it boiled down to a simple little sentence right away. I've had time to play with it since then. A girl's gotta brand.)

So with that in mind, was this Oprah dream inspiring me to actually do *that* to the best of my ability?

Nope.

And here's the kicker: It had actually done the opposite. I was putting so much mental energy into trying to be discovered that I wasn't actually doing the work that was worth discovering. Following the dream had become more of a distraction than an inspiration. I wasn't putting my all into figuring out how to move to fulfill my dreams. I wasn't actually doing "the work."

Notice I didn't say that I wasn't doing *any* work. I was working pretty hard actually. At my jobs and at angling and at getting myself in the right position for that dream. *But the work you do in pursuit of a dream isn't necessarily the work that serves your highest and best use.* I was working to achieve something that I hoped would *then* allow me to experience fulfillment and purpose. And that's a terrible waste of a life.

If my life were to end today, would I want to be known as a person who was trying to be Oprah? Or would I want to be known as actually being me, in my own world, in my own way?

QUESTION 4: What can this new story look like for me?

Once I finally came to this realization, after months and months of wrestling with these ideas, I decided that my new story wouldn't be about pursuing, chasing, or following *anything*. It would be about *doing*. About creating habits that allowed me to be productive and empowered right now, not just in pursuit of a far-off fantasy. It's really all about shifting focus to one simple question: *How now?* How can I do this thing that fulfills my purpose and healthy desires now?

How now is actionable. It gives you a vision of a life that doesn't depend on variables that are beyond your control, and it leaves open room for future unknowns. It gives you the space to create and respond to your current circumstances rather than getting caught up in feelings of longing, disappointment, and failure. It's the "what" companion to the "why" of your dreams.

As I took this approach with all of my dreams, a simple exercise started to emerge:

Whenever I would think of a dream and what it was that I was actually seeking from it, I would use my story smart lens to assess the true desires and motivations behind it, which usually only took a little bit of digging. Once I figured it out, I unpacked and addressed any unhealthy stories (like the "validation as success" story I found hidden in the Oprah dream). Then I removed them from the equation to see what was left. If nothing remained, if the entire dream was based on stories that didn't align with my values, I eliminated the dream altogether.

But if there was some good left there, something that hinted at what I could and should be doing to make my life better, I simply asked, "How now?" How could I achieve this dream now? How could I fulfill right now the purpose that this dream is meant to bring into my life? *If I stopped the chase and only had today to feel the feeling that I had hoped this dream would bring me, what would I be doing?*

And voilà! I'd make myself a promise to spend more time *doing that* than I had spent thinking about the dream.

Here's what that looks like in practice:

A dream is to be a *New York Times* bestselling author.

What's underneath the dream?

1. A desire for acclaim and approval

2. A desire to publish important work

I can assess that my desire for acclaim isn't particularly important to my values, but the desire to publish important things that touch many lives points me toward my work.

How now? I can write a book that is meaningful to me, that I can be proud of, and try to get it in the hands of as many people who need to hear the message as possible.

A dream is to have two children, a boy and a girl.

What's underneath the dream?

1. A desire for the "perfect" family

2. A desire to give children love and pass on all that I have to them, leaving a legacy and building amazing little world-changers

I know that there *is* no perfect family and that gender has nothing to do with the value of my future children. On top of that, my biology

is the ultimate decider of how, when, what, and even *if* it will repro-
duce. But the second desire? I can do that no matter what.

How now? Of course, LB and I can begin trying to have children
however we want when we're ready, but we can also mentor young
people who are *already here* and in need of that kind of love and wisdom right now.

A dream is to have a million dollars.

What's underneath the dream?

1. A belief that wealth will make me happy

2. A desire to be financially secure

I can assess that an expectation of money bringing me happiness
doesn't match my values, but a desire to be financially secure points
me toward very clear work.

How now? I can begin making the choices that increase my
income and help me feel financial peace and stability right now. I can
also seek help—an accountant, a financial planner, a mentor—to help
me better understand money and plan for my future.

———

Simply identifying what it was that I felt compelled to do, and why,
meant that I could *immediately* begin orienting my days around fulfilling that purpose. Knowing this gave me more excitement about waking up every day than a dream of fame or material wealth ever could.

I stopped evaluating opportunities in the light of whether or not
they would set me up to reach a dream, and instead became obsessed
with the knowledge that I could impact so many more people walking
in purpose today than I could by hoping and waiting to reach millions
in the future.

These three examples are simply ones that come to mind for me and for a lot of my friends. But the exercise works no matter what your dreams are.

———

It takes narrative intelligence for any of us to resist the seduction of the "follow your dreams" story and instead say, "That is a story that is made to keep me in a constant state of pursuit and longing."

The emphasis that society has placed on our dreams is out of whack with the value that dreams should actually have in your life. Because if we accept the story that dreams should be our primary motivation and we pursue them without any narrative intelligence, they can turn into nightmares, taunting us and distracting us from who we are, what we are put on this earth to do, and what beautiful future is truly best for us.

If you dig to find out the underlying motivation, desire, or reasoning behind each dream that you are following, you'll get a clear sense of what would *actually* sustain you and inspire you to get up each and every day and do the work that you need to do.

As for what that work is, don't get hung up on the word "purpose." Maybe you prefer to think of it as a mission, an important assignment. Perhaps the word "calling" suits you better. On my podcast *The Called Life*, I speak to mission-driven women who feel pulled by and toward something greater than themselves. These are accomplished, wildly successful women, many of whom are living lives that others only dream about. And, surprisingly enough, not one of them in three seasons of the show has talked about "following their dreams." They all have talked about a sense of purpose, a feeling that there is a task they must do. And that drive has led them to high places and a sense of fulfillment that is less about chasing something and more about *being* something.

Whatever that something is for you, don't get stuck on trying to come up with the perfect answer. If we take the time to listen to our hearts and review our life—our talents, what brings us joy, what matters most to us, where we feel the most useful—we all have some inkling, some best guess of what that is.

Remember: There is no immediately visible "right" path. Instead, you should be finding and designing your life in a responsive and fluid way. Understanding your highest and best use is a process. You won't wake up one day with a simple sentence or a tagline or even the vision of the perfect job for you. You may have to dig to uncover it.

Michelangelo believed that every block of stone had a statue inside it and it was his task as the sculptor to set it free, to chisel away until the sculpture presented itself. And therein lies the difference between following a dream and walking in purpose: Dreaming is fantasizing about the vision of a final sculpture that is like another sculpture you once saw elsewhere. But chiseling as often as you can, with your best effort to create something new, even if you have no idea what the final result will look like, simply because you feel compelled to chisel and create, is the work of purpose. And it is the work that yields masterpieces.

YOUR TURN: HOW NOW, FOR YOU?

Now we can use our story smarts to uncover the true impact of stories on our lives and choose to place our attention where it counts. What are the dreams that you've been following, looking at every day, and holding on to tightly as signals of your future success? Go ahead and ask "How now?" for each and every one of them.

This new narrative has the potential to change your life immediately. And the icing on the cake is that it could take you to a lofty, prosperous place far beyond what your limited mind thought to put on your Pinterest wall or write in your journal fifteen years ago.

"How now?" points you toward the life you are capable of living and creating right this very instant. No matter your resources, no matter your title, no matter your privilege each day, tomorrow is not promised. Hope is not a strategy. With this mind-set, you can do, say, or make things that help people survive, thrive, and change the world, without hoping for some material metric of validation or success. Your days will have a purpose that is dependent on no one but you.

The truth is, I will never stop dreaming entirely. Every now and then I still let myself fantasize about the big house, the high income, and the glamorous life. And Oprah, if you're reading this, please do feel free to slide all the way into my DMs. I'm sure we could still find tons to talk about.

But today, in place of my vision board, I have a simple printout of this quote from the divine Arundhati Roy's *The God of Small Things*:

> *The only dream worth having is to dream that you will live while you are alive, and die only when you are dead. To love, to be loved. To never forget your own insignificance. To never get used to the unspeakable violence and vulgar disparity of the life around you. To seek joy in the saddest places. To pursue beauty to its lair. To never simplify what is complicated or complicate what is simple. To respect strength, never power. Above all to watch. To try and understand. To never look away. And never, never to forget.*

That is now my greatest dream. And to it I say, how now?

OLD STORY: Follow your dreams.

TRUE STORY: Pursue purpose and ask, "How now?"

CHAPTER 6

THE STORY OF WORK

Work, work, work, work, work, work
You see me I be work, work, work, work, work, work
—RIHANNA

As much as I was enjoying wrestling with the major philosoph-
ical questions in my life—figuring out my purpose, experimenting with my path, practicing bravery—there was one reality that
I just could not ignore: Mama needed a job. Not necessarily a job-job,
but at the very least, a new something to wake me up each day. A
career. A type of work that I felt was worthy of this new life and as
far as possible from the social impact rat race that I had previously
been a part of.

Taking consulting gigs, waiting for freelance checks to come in,
doing one-off trainings, I felt out of place, useless, and unimportant. Sure I was busy—I had to be in order to maintain some sense of
financial stability. But for the first time, I had no clear vision of who I
was in the world if not . . . a worker. Who was I with no title, no staff,
no people asking to meet with me? Who was I without a clear project
to work toward, a clear vision of my professional goals?

I have *always* been a worker. At home, at school, at church, even
in my parents' offices. As a little girl, I would sit outside of my moth-

er's office, at her secretary Miss Vivian's desk, and "organize" her supplies. Miss Vivian would sometimes reward me with a few dollars. But even when she didn't, the hugs and kisses were enough for me. If there was a task, I was going to complete it, give my all to it and hopefully get some praise or love in return.

As I grew up, the sense of identity and worth that I got from any of my jobs mattered just as much to me as the paychecks I was bringing home each week. According to the adults around me who marveled at my work ethic, I was a "model young person" simply because I worked and worked well. I had always valued the praise that I would get for working hard. But once I became an adult, I realized I could make money at the same time. I was killing all of the birds with one stone. Work was from then on out my happy place.

To tell you the truth, I have always felt like I could be good at almost anything. I know that sounds arrogant, but growing up in a small church, I learned how to slide easily into any role that needed to be filled. So when I entered the work world, I assumed that the same principle applied: I was supposed to work hard where work needed to be done, and do it well. That attitude had become a part of my identity.

It made me somewhat of a shape-shifter. While I was in college, I worked full-time at Aveda Bethesda, a ritzy spa in the wealthy suburbs of Maryland, and because I have such a strong can-do, full-throttle work ethic, in just six months I went from being the young girl behind the cash register to managing the store. The customers loved me. They would ask specifically to work with me, and I loved helping make these older women feel better about themselves. I knew *nothing* about makeup (and still don't), but somehow I was performing full makeup applications. The owner of the spa saw such potential in me that she offered me an apprenticeship where I could train to become an aesthetician. The next thing I knew, I was learning to give facials, and bikini waxes in the shape of lightning bolts, to the Washington Redskins cheerleaders. Despite going to school full-time for African American Studies and Public Policy, I studied my aesthetics materials and took my Aveda classes so seriously that I began seeing running a spa in my future. For no other reason than the fact that I was addicted to the high of "crushing it" at work.

When I graduated college, I had no idea what to do with my degree, but I needed a job and I needed one quickly. I had a wonderful professor who was willing to help me out and hooked me up with a civil rights organization that fell in line with my values. So there I was, one of the few candidates that had never had an internship, who knew absolutely nothing about politics or social justice. Yet I knew in my heart I could do the job anyway. I talked my way through the interview, got the job, and kicked into high gear.

From that job, two years later I was recruited to be the director of policy at the millennial arm of Washington's most powerful liberal think tank. This was what one might call my professional "come up." I was now running national voting campaigns, making guest appearances on TV, organizing projects with young people on over five hundred campuses, raising millions of dollars, and enjoying unprecedented access to powerful leaders, all while advocating for progressive policy change on behalf of young people. By the time I was twenty-five, I was the face of Generation Progress, appearing on stage with Bill Clinton, sitting next to Bill Maher on HBO, and running all over the world telling the stories of millennials who were demanding change in their communities.

I hustled, worked around the clock, racked up awards, compliments, and consistent—if meager—paychecks. That pattern continued for years, through several more high-profile roles. Until . . . the mic drop.

I was exhausted from living on that kind of autopilot, do-whatever-it-takes-to-get-the-job-done overdrive. And after running myself into the ground for over a decade, I felt like I had nothing to show for it. Well, not *nothing*. Just nothing that made me happy.

In the past, I had always tried to figure out how the opportunity that was in front of me could work, rather than seeking opportunities that were in fact the best for me. Now that I was searching for a new life, the messages from the world were ringing loudly in my ears. I was surrounded by the "Do what you love and love what you do!" mantra. Was I "following my bliss"? Should I let my passion be my paycheck? Or should I find something lucrative, work hard, and use my talents as a means to an end?

To make some decisions, I would first need to unpack these slogans about work and the stories that had created them.

QUESTION 1: What is the story?

For the most part, our society defines work as what we do with our capacity to make a living. It is how we make money and it's how we spend a big chunk of our most valuable asset: time.

Along the way to the working world, we receive loud lessons about the value of work and, ultimately, our value in relation to it. Culturally speaking, work is a huge, if not defining, characteristic of who we are and who we think we should be in the world. How hard we work, how much we work, where we work, how much we are paid for it . . . with that much emphasis on work, it is hard to separate yourself and your identity from it.

I'm sure you've heard the mother of all work stories: Aesop's fable about the ant and the grasshopper. The grasshopper spent all his time singing while the ant was working hard. In the end, the grasshopper was left dying of hunger while getting scolded by the smug, hard-working ant. The moral of the story was clear: The harder you work, the better off you will be.

The idea of a strong work ethic (which in the professional world is often code for "how much work can be sucked out of this person beyond the baseline that the company is paying for") has long been associated with integrity and morality. Hard work is a virtue, they say, but no one really tells us why. It just is. Our puritanical obsession with work is on display everywhere in popular culture, from athletics to movies and music. We idolize the hard worker and applaud his or her character. This idea morphs quite easily into a tool for judging the character and integrity of others. The deeper your work ethic and the harder you work, the better a person we presume you are. And if you aren't working hard, you deserve the life of poverty you have brought upon yourself. Shame on you!

It's as though work has some mysterious, inherent value, but if you look closer, you'll realize that really, the value of your work in society's eyes is very simple: money.

That part of the story begins your first day of school, because let's face it, in many ways, going to school is our very first job. It's the place where we're supposed to work as hard as we can for six to eight hours a day, and the ultimate reward of years and years of hard work is . . . drumroll please . . . a career! If we do our best and work not just for the sake or joy of learning, but to get good grades, that will propel us into even better schools that will spit us out into a career that can sustain us and, hopefully, help us earn back some of what society (or our parents) spent educating us.

The narrative we were taught is clear: Hard work is key to all success. If you work hard, you'll get ahead. Hard work is the secret sauce that leads to money; hard work is the vaccine for poverty. If you're financially insecure, it must mean that somewhere along the way, whether in school or in the workforce, you just didn't work hard enough, right?

Now, you and I both know—I hope—that that's not true. The story is broken. There are plenty of good people who are working really hard and not reaping rewards that are commensurate with their efforts. The Congressional Budget Office describes the average minimum wage worker as full-time and thirty-five years old, and because minimum wage is not the same as a living wage, many of them are working multiple jobs to make ends meet. Their financial situation is more a reflection of how America *places a value on* their work than a result of how hard they are actually working.

Hard work simply does not guarantee success, however you define it. That does not mean that hard work is a bad thing. But there is no guarantee of a materially abundant outcome. Think of it like the scientific paradigm of necessity and sufficiency. You may need an egg to make a cake—an egg is necessary—but an egg alone is insufficient: Having an egg does not mean you will have a cake. It's the same way with hard work. For most of us (except those who are extraordinarily lucky and are handed a fortune on a silver platter), hard work is a necessary but not sufficient condition to success. There are many other factors that go into the mix: timing, talent and skill, geography, the economy, supply and demand, relationships, and luck. But because so many of those factors are outside of our sphere of influence, we double down on the one we think we can control. We work harder and harder and more and more, hoping that all this effort will pay off in the end.

In the story where hard work is a virtue, a reflection of our character, a demonstration of how we use our education, the descriptor and the supposed predictor of our future success and fortune, it is easy to see work as the most important thing about our identity and lives. So it's no surprise that we don't talk about our work as something that we do but as who we are. All adults know how to answer this question, even when they are faking it: I *am* a _____ (fill in the blank applicable to your job identity).

But what happens when you are laid off, fired, or unable to work in the way that you want? Losing a job happens all the time. And the result is often a sense of depression, self-loathing, and emotional insecurity that is just as impactful as financial insecurity.

The Perfect Gig

But that's not all there is to the work story we've been taught. Our generation has, for some reason, added even more pressure to the mix. Millennials now fetishize a particular type of work. In short, work has to be . . . amazing.

So many of us have lists of the qualities of a dream job: Flexible work hours. Ability to work from home or anywhere in the world. Incorporates lifetime passions. Offers full benefits. Competitive salary. Is socially responsible. Provides part ownership. Provides learning and travel opportunities. Rapid growth potential. Pays for graduate school or repays student loans. Offers mentorship. Changes the world.

For our generation, the expectations aren't just about how hard you work, but what that work is supposed to be. Long gone are the days when just having employment that allowed you to take care of your family without wanting to die from sheer boredom was enough. Now our job is supposed to be fun, fulfilling, meaningful, and *cool*. In fact, it shouldn't even feel like work.

That's the guidance of most career coaching today. A quick Google search turns up the following headlines:

"When Work Doesn't Feel Like Work: 6 Signs You Are Doing What You Love"

"Do What You Love and You'll Never Work Another Day in Your Life"

"How to Find a Job That Doesn't Feel Like Work"

On top of this, we are rewriting the rules of the workplace. The most desirable work situation has become one where there's no separation between your work life and personal life, between your passions and how you make a living. We saw our parents' generation live stoic lives, working for thirty years in jobs they hated, and we refuse to do the same. We are going to find joy and love and satisfaction in our professional lives if it kills us.

If we look at social media, it seems like finding that job should be easy to do. How hard can it be to craft a work life that blends seamlessly with one's personal life? That lets you be your best self, 24/7? We live in a world where just being visible can make you millions. (Hello, Kim K.) On Instagram, people build entire careers off of their lifestyle and call it being an "influencer," as in: "I work out all the time and I'm really, really pretty, so let me post a bunch of pictures of me working out and talking about working hard, and then I can build a whole business off of being a workout goddess just by living my life and taking pictures of my life. See how natural and effortless this is?"

If it sounds like I'm hating, I'm not. Kudos to anyone who has been able to make a living this way. "Social media influencer" has become a viable career path. Buyer beware, though: Many people who appear to be doing it successfully are actually not. I often hear of influencers posting fake ads on Instagram, pretending to have endorsement deals and brand partnerships that don't yet exist in order to actually attract real ones. So your favorite model who you think is being paid to pitch flat tummy tea may not only not actually be drinking it, she probably isn't getting paid to pretend that she does. She just wants you to think that she is. Weird, right? It's a cycle just like most others: *fake it till you make it.* The industry just hasn't been around long enough for us to see what actually happens to those who don't make it. Good luck and Godspeed.

But regardless of whether your job is online or offline, life hack gurus encourage us to spend as little time as possible doing the work that *does* feel like work. Maybe just four hours a week, in fact. If we're working too hard, we're not working smart, which is very confusing. Aren't we also supposed to be working as hard as humanly possible to be considered virtuous and valuable? So we should be working really hard, but like, only four hours a week? And if you look at your current life and find that's not the case, perhaps the nine-to-five life isn't for you at all. Maybe you should try an entirely different approach . . . they say. Maybe you should be an entrepreneur.

Boss Up

The *do what you love, love what you do* narrative coupled with a difficult economy that has made employment less reliable has caused many of us to jump headfirst into the world of entrepreneurship. A study out of Bentley University suggests that the majority of us believe that career success will ultimately *require* us to be entrepreneurial. In fact, 67 percent of the young adults surveyed had goals of entrepreneurship.

Here's the subtext for the entrepreneurial narrative: Having a job means "working for someone else's dream," and why would anyone in their right mind want to do that? We have glorified entrepreneurship with shows like *Shark Tank*, cute motivational titles like *Girlboss*, and an entire cottage industry of online marketers who have built businesses telling other people how to build an online business.

How many times have you started a business? Or planned to start a business? Or written out the ideas for your own business? Or ordered business cards and built a personal website? Now tell me how many of those businesses are actually up and running today? None? Don't feel attacked. I have been there. All it means is that you too have, at one point or another, been seduced by the siren call of entrepreneurship.

I have always been the official Queen of Side Gigs and Business Ventures. I am entrepreneurial by nature. And while yes, that has often led me to be successfully self-employed, running my own business, so many of my mistakes, false starts, time wasting, and premature decisions in the past happened because I felt culturally pressured into starting my own thing, whether or not I was prepared, had a great idea, or even knew exactly what it was that I wanted to be doing.

If we aren't able to be a boss, at the very least we all must have a side hustle, the *thing* that we do outside of our *main thing*. These days, it's practically mandatory. I know doctors who have websites selling homemade body butters and—I lie to you not—a PhD student teaching physics by day and working at Chipotle by night. Sometimes it's a matter of survival to piece together low wages. But other times, we do it because of the culture that makes us feel as if we must all be working *more*. Especially if we can find in a side gig the joy that's lacking from our main gig.

QUESTION 2: Does this story serve my values and me?

So how did we get here? Why has work become the story that is supposed to reflect who we are and bring us independence, happiness, and fulfillment in a way that used to be relegated to other aspects of our lives, like family and relationships?

First, as our economy changed over the past hundred years, we actually began to spend way more time working, feeding the beast of capitalism. According to the Economic Policy Institute, wages have remained stagnant over the past forty years, while the cost of education and living continues to rise. In other words, we're working more to make less. And it's not just hard cash that we're getting less of: We've lost job security, retirement, pensions, and worse still, health coverage.

For some of us, the work never stops. We stay late at the office, then check on our work email like it's a newborn baby, making sure that we always know what's going on and are available if needed. And in an increasingly mobile and global society, work often takes us away from our community. As we began to move away from home to find work, we made a life around our jobs. The things we used to define happiness and joy by, like friends and family, are no longer what surrounds us. So if you're trying to hold on to some semblance of sanity or find joy in what you spend the majority of your time doing, you're going to have to look at work.

Now let me be clear: I'm not making fun of people who want work to spark joy. Of course we should want that! A lot of what we desire and expect is actually shaping the workforce to be healthier, more socially responsible, and more sustainable. Plus, as far as I'm concerned, we should be demanding every. single. thing. that we can get out of The Man, since The Man never hesitates to demand every. single. thing. from us. But the danger with this story comes, as most things do, when we hold up a vague idea as an ideal. When our realities and the prototype don't match, we rarely place 100 percent of the blame on the job or the society that hasn't caught up to our dream. Instead, many of us do this weird thing where we feel ashamed of not having been smart or savvy or talented or *something* enough to have manifested our dream professional lives. We feel "less than" because our professional lives don't look like the ones we see in magazines or on Facebook. And that feeling doesn't serve any of us.

I was so frustrated by this dynamic that one afternoon, I did what any modern person does when he or she has a deep insight: I wrote a Facebook status.

PSA: You don't have to travel all the time, work from home, be on TV, work for a "movement" or lead (what looks like) a passion-filled, independent life to 1. make a difference 2. be valuable 3. walk in your purpose. And I HATE the cultural narrative that makes you feel like you do. I love that y'all find my life and the lives of some of my "fancy" friends inspiring (according to a lot of the messages I get) but in case that inspiration ever makes you feel less than—because social media is really good at that—just

a reminder: Your lives are inspiring too. To me. To your parents.
To your children. To people who you may not even know. You
take care of your families. You help people. You brighten people's
days. You work hard. You're smart. You're creative. You're tal-
ented. And you add something to the world. Period. Don't get
sucked into this Fast Company *narrative that jet-setting "entre-*
preneurs" and so-called "dream followers" make the world go
'round. That's hype. We are all necessary. Please appreciate your-
self no matter what your 9-5 is.

I logged off and didn't think anything of it. I had gotten the
thought off my chest and hoped that a few people would read it and
feel good. I had no idea just how much it would resonate. I logged
back on an hour later and saw hundreds of comments. And the comments themselves were pretty telling.

"E—Thank You. I second-guess my choices all the time
because I see the amazing things that you're doing at work
and wonder where I went wrong."

"OMG This. This. This. I'm embarrassed to post things about
work on here because I feel like a loser."

"Can I show this post to my friends? Us 9-5ers never get any
love."

My friends and followers let me know that somewhere along
the way, while celebrating dream jobs and nontraditional work
lives, we've made a lot of other people feel like crap. We share condescending memes about "settling" for "regular jobs" under the
pretense of trying to inspire. But the truth is, everyone's life is different. And there is no objectively better or worse work life as it
pertains to your value in the world. We are all just doing the absolute best we can.

My mother, who comes from a generation of women who did what they had to do, looks at me and my younger sister with part fascination, part humor, and part awe. She just can't imagine having the type of expectations that we have for work and thinks that we are both blessed and cursed to have them. She's right.

All of these narratives combine to teach us one big, meta story: *Work is a status symbol.* What it is, how much someone is willing to pay you for it, how long you spend doing it, and what you get out of it all determines how you are perceived in the world and is a reflection of where you belong in society.

But these stories about work have failed us. In our quest to live up to them we are suffering from burnout, being overworked and underpaid, and living with constant anxiety around who we are if we don't have the perfect job and who we could be if we dared to try something different.

QUESTION 3: What if I believed something else?

Once I recognized the colossal sham that this story is, I could at least look at my future through a new lens. Even though I was still overwhelmed by options and determined to make my next move even better than all the ones that had come before it, I was going to rethink work and my relationship to it, for the long haul.

I love language. I think a lot about the usage, meaning, and hidden power that words have over how we think and act. So when I started to think deeply about work, I uncovered a pretty notable insight.

Have you ever noticed how people use the words "work" and "job" as if they were interchangeable? When we leave our house in the morning to go to our *job* we say, "I'm on my way to *work*!" As we leave the office we say, "I'm getting off of *work*." And because *work* is synonymous with employment, we call the *jobless* "out of *work*."

But the truth is, these two words are actually not the same.

A job is what you do to make *money*. It connects your time and your skills to a worldly, material system—an organization, an institution, a product or service, or at the very least, a scale of compensation. It keeps you accountable to someone or something, and work is what is asked of you in return for financial gain.

A job also has parameters. It begins and it ends. It can be good, it can be bad, and, above all, nearly every part of it is susceptible to factors not within your control. A job's value is determined by the market and the increments of productivity that the market sets. Society decides if you're working hard enough based on how well you do your job and how much material gain you have to show for it. You don't determine the availability or sustainability of jobs, and you don't control how much a job is worth. And a job does not define you.

Our work, on the other hand, is what we do to make *meaning*. To be useful. To express ourselves. To contribute to what we believe matters. Your work is all of the ways that you put your effort and your heart toward what matters to you, for reasons that are bigger and deeper than money. Your work is the mental, physical, emotional labor that you choose to give to the world. You decide where, for whom, and with whom you work. And the "why" of your work is not determined by the economy or a market. Work is the thing that you would do for free, even if no one wanted to pay you for it. And in my new story, no one determines the value, the dignity, or the nature of my work—of my time and talents and sweat and energy—but me.

Most of us work quite a bit outside of our jobs. We work in our homes, in our communities, in our places of worship, and in our relationships. We work on our health, our emotions, and our hobbies. We work in our kitchens, our gardens, and in the gym. So what if I allowed this distinction to guide my thinking? What would the impact be?

First, I would know that regardless of what's happening in the world, regardless of the market or the economy, regardless of whether I take a job that isn't perfect for me or lose one that I thought was, I won't lose my identity and my sense of peace and pride in who I am based on the outcome of any one job. Letting that happen would be as silly as judging who you are based on traffic. I can navigate traffic, I can try to "beat" traffic, and every day I can do my best to move safely and swiftly through it. But I do not control traffic. And traffic is not a reflection of me. Similarly, you can't judge who I am, my talents, or my character based off of a job. Because I do not control a job or a market.

This distinction was a game changer for me.

QUESTION 4: What can this new story look like for me?

Once I understood the difference between a job and work, I felt like someone had told me I could bring an extra carry-on onto the plane. Up until this point, I had spent hours trying to pack everything I owned into one tiny suitcase. My passions, my priorities, my talents, my financial needs, my values, my identity, my desire to change the world, my lifestyle goals—all of it into one small roller bag marked J-O-B. I felt guilty when I couldn't get it all in and frustrated at the thought of everything that I owned and all of who I am being squeezed into that one bag. When the bag finally broke, I thought that I would have to replace it or I just wouldn't be able to fly.

But now, with my new story, there were *two* bags that I could fit my pursuits in. And better yet, no one could tell me how to pack them. I could put some of my passions in one bag and some of my passions in the other. I could make one bag be all about my purpose, and still have one bag to carry the skills that would get me paid. I knew that there would be times when I would want one bag to fit inside the other so I could carry all the same items together. And there would be other times when I would only fit the absolute basics and a few important priorities (like the need to make money or support my family) into the job bag, with everything else going into the work case.

Either a job or work can be in service of your purpose.

Either a job or work can be in service of a pleasure or passion.

Either a job or work can be in service of a life responsibility.

And either a job or work can change at any given time.

Neither has to be everything all the time. And there is no judgment or shame inherent in however you choose to give your time to your job or your work.

There are things that I sometimes have to do that have no greater meaning for me than to earn money, like consulting. I don't love it, but I do it when I need an additional stream of income or if I see a particularly lucrative opportunity. If clients stopped working with me or no one thought my skills as a consultant were incredibly valuable anymore, I wouldn't be crushed. Because consulting is a job-only activity.

And then there is the work that is just work. Music is a great example. Singing is a passion. I love it and am good at it. But I have never wanted to be a professional singer. I never wanted that part of my life to become tainted by the pressures of trying to make money or making my gift susceptible to what others want from me. It's too sacred to me. I just want to use it to experience joy—alone, with God, and with my family. That is my absolute highest bliss, and I have no need for it to intersect whatsoever with how I make money. So I continue to work—put lots of effort—into my singing for no other reason than I care about it.

Then there are the pursuits that are *both* work and job. My writing, speaking, teaching, making content, helping people, translating big ideas into understandable ones, fighting for justice, are all things that I *work* hard at doing well. I would work in these ways whether or not anyone paid me to. They bring me joy, they take advantage of my talent, they help me fulfill my purpose in the world. It just so happens that I have crafted a professional life where I can also get paid to do these things and they are my job.

Can you see the difference?

In the end, I knew that I wanted to use my voice, my media savvy, and my expertise in politics, culture, and spirituality to lift up alternative ideas of how to live and make the world a better place. That's where this book comes in, and it's what I'm now doing as both my work and my job. But who knows what the future holds, for me or for you.

YOUR TURN: DEFINING YOURSELF AND YOUR WORK

There are a million and one pieces of career advice floating around in the atmosphere nowadays. Each one will tell you how to find a great job or achieve whatever professional goals you may have. There are checklists and Listservs and "best practices" for discovering the best job fit and work path for you. And you know what? Many of them will help. But none of them will lead you to the thing that you're actually searching for: a whole life where you feel peace and pride in your pursuits. That will require a new story, one that is true for you.

Your job may eventually merge with your life's purpose or passions, or maybe it won't. Your most meaningful work could link to your income, or maybe it never will. Your passions and priorities may change and your job most certainly will. But you won't find true contentment and fulfillment until you break free from the stories of work that have guided your chase of the perfect job, that have shamed you for where and how you choose to work, and that have caused you to work yourself nearly to death for a system that isn't working for you.

You are more than your job. You are more than what you contribute to the economy and what title other people have put on your pursuits. You are a work of art, and your greatest responsibility is to use your efforts in the way most worthwhile for your values.

If you have been led to believe that your job is the greatest contribution you make to the world, think again. It isn't. *You are.* And rejecting any story that says otherwise is something worth working toward.

OLD STORY: Work is a status symbol.

TRUE STORY: Our job is how we make a living.
Our work is how we build a life.

CHAPTER 7

THE STORY OF MONEY

But everybody's like Cristal, Maybach,
diamonds on your timepiece . . .
That kind of lux just ain't for us
—LORDE, "ROYALS"

Lorde's song "Royals" was one of the most popular songs of 2013 for a reason. And not just because I personally played it 9 million times on Spotify. It felt like a generational anthem for people who grew up with wealth and materialism being shoved down their throats weekly on *Cribs* and the Real Housewives of Everywhere. The song was an exhale for people who just wanted to be honest about what they had and where they were from. And although Lorde is closer to my younger sister's age than to mine, it felt like she wrote the song just for me. It perfectly summed up my exhaustion with a culture of money obsession that promoted anxiety, shame, and pretense.

At the same time as that song topped the charts, my money anxiety was at its peak. Where was my next check going to come from? Why didn't I have enough savings to fall back on? Should my next move be strictly a money play to make up for all the years of working in nonprofits? At my age, shouldn't I be in a better financial position than this? Was it bad that I still loved Walmart? What would people think if they found out that I was depending on LB to pay the bills while I figured out my life? When people asked if I had taken time off to "travel," what would they think if they knew the real reason behind my no was that I couldn't afford to go anywhere?

By the time they were my age, my parents and aunts and uncles had children, cars, and homes of their own. I could pretty much only afford the car. Sometimes, I'd find myself wallowing in self-pity, feeling as if everyone else had a surplus of money. My lack of disposable income and the stress that I felt maintaining a basic adult life with student debt and a stagnant income in this unforgiving economy made me feel ashamed to have so much less than my more privileged peers. Other times, when I had a reality check and remembered those who had so much less than me, especially friends of mine or members of my extended family, I felt even more ashamed for daring to complain about my "First World problems."

All of my feelings of shame around my finances were bubbling over. I was so tired of having this complicated, anxiety-filled relationship with money, because I'd had it my whole life. From the time I was a little girl, I had occupied a weird middle ground of not poor enough to legitimately complain but not rich enough to feel completely at ease.

As a young professional, it seemed as if everyone assumed I was well off because I could afford to work in the nonprofit world and was traveling to fancy conferences. In the rarified air that I was working in, there were a lot of people my age who'd come from very privileged backgrounds. I apparently hadn't gotten the memo that the meager salaries in the not-for-profit world were really meant for people who already were swimming in profit.

So the truth is that I wasn't poor, but like a lot of millennials, I was what we call cash-poor. I made enough to pay my rent, I had good benefits, I could afford a gym membership and on good months some cable, but that was about it. It wasn't a luxurious lifestyle and I was fine with that, yet I always felt as if I had done something wrong.

I saw so many people living *The Life*. Taking vacations, paying for the hottest new workout membership at $250/month, not getting angry at paying an even split of the bill for a meal with friends at which they had only ordered an appetizer and a glass of water. My pockets weren't evolved enough yet to let that last one slide.

And therein lies the inevitable onslaught of shame: How come I was so smart but I didn't know how to make a lot of money? How come I didn't have as much as people expected me to have? What had I done wrong?

To be honest, my deepest desires for more money had nothing to do with greed or materialism. Many of my dreams—and the shame that came when I couldn't realize them—were about taking care of the people that I loved.

I want a big house to invite people to stay with me whenever they need a place to stay.

I want to send my aunt Kim and uncle Ronnie on their dream vacation to Italy.

I want to pay off and gloriously remodel every inch of my mother's home, especially her garden and deck.

I want to pay off my sister's student loans, give her a wad of cash, and let her pursue her passions with no worries.

I want to set up my future children with such a safety net that they can be little Jaden and Willow Smiths—rich, quirky, and free.

I didn't yet have enough to do any of those things, but I had enough to be okay and sometimes more than okay. I know what it's like to give a gift of $1,000—the check that I saved up to help my sister pay for her study abroad trip—and also what it's like to have your debit card declined for a $10 meal right before payday. I know what it's like to sleep in a five-star hotel in Dubai, paid for by the

World Economic Forum, while hoping your landlord hasn't noticed that your rent is ten days late.

You wouldn't know it to look at me because I hide it well and let the shame eat me up inside. And I know that I'm not alone. For so many of us, the narratives surrounding money are long and complicated. They are intertwined with the stories of race and gender and family and luck and tragedy and history.

Maybe you have never had to worry about money in your entire life.

Maybe you have always felt resentful toward those who have so much simply by virtue of where, when, and to whom they were born (privilege is a hell of a thing).

Maybe you have been a notoriously poor manager of your money (Anyone owe hundreds of dollars in parking tickets just because you keep forgetting to pay them? No? Just me?).

Maybe you were fine and then one unforeseen event—a layoff, an illness, a family emergency—took it all away.

Maybe you have more than enough but are addicted to shopping and spending.

Maybe not an hour goes by when you're not thinking about money.

I don't know your particular story, but here's what I do know: According to data from a 2017 report by GoBankingRates.com, about one in four Americans said that money is the thing they think about most on a daily basis. Thirty-four percent have no savings at all. Young African Americans have only 10 percent of the savings of other races, and both young blacks and young Latinos earn almost half of what young white people earn. And not many young people, regardless of race, earn that much to begin with. Millennial net worth is *half* as much as boomers were worth when they were the same age. In other words, not a lot of us are living the baller lives we see on TV or even the ones that we hoped to live when we dreamed about our adult futures.

We are generally struggling economically, and dealing with greater income inequality than any generation before. We are really drowning in debt, and spending a huge chunk of our income on housing. We do not have much to show in terms of savings or retirement accounts for all our hard work. In fact, many of us don't have any assets and can't afford good health care. The limits on wage growth make social mobility far harder now than it ever was in our grandparents' and parents' generations.

Those sobering realities exist in direct opposition to a world of *shoulds* that are haunting us around every corner. The shoulds are a part of society's narrative, and the shoulds about money are everywhere.

You should have two times your annual income in savings by the time you're thirty-five.

You should spend no more than one-third of your income on rent.

You should not carry a lot of debt.

You should have perfect credit scores.

You should have high credit limits on your credit cards, and yet not use more money than you can pay back every month.

The shoulds around money are even more extensive for women. We're not supposed to demand money, negotiate, or ask for it directly. Women who do that with their partners are called ruthless gold diggers. In the office, they are labeled as entitled, ambitious climbers.

When reality doesn't meet the shoulds, as it so often doesn't in our current economy, it's the recipe for shame. And anyone can feel it. An *Atlantic* article entitled "The Secret Shame of Middle Class Americans" reported that 47 percent of middle-class Americans would have trouble finding $400 for an emergency. They would either have to sell something or they just wouldn't be able to come up with it.

The shame around money narratives show up when we have:

Shame for not being able to spoil our loved ones.

Shame for being perceived as less than responsible.

Shame for not having made our talent or skill pay handsomely.

Shame for having debt.

Shame for not having an emergency fund.

Shame for being so preoccupied with money.

Shame for wanting it so desperately.

There's a reason why we're not supposed to talk openly and extensively about money. A telltale sign of shame is secrecy. We've been taught that talking about money is not appropriate. Or classy. It's too revealing. Too intimate. Too rude. We're not supposed to tell people how much we make, or how much debt we have, or how much the super-awesome thing we just bought costs. We know almost nothing about anyone else's actual financial state, yet we measure ourselves against one another's perceived situation. And then comes shame's first cousin, pretense.

Here's how it works: There's a perception (partially supported by society's stories, partially created in your own mind by shame's second cousin, envy) that you should have something that you don't— a material good, a lifestyle, some other marker of economic status.

Rather than admit you can't have it, you buy into that perception and feel like you have to pretend you can afford it.

Those of us who live on the internet call it "stunting on the 'gram," which basically means posting things on social media that make it look like you have more money than you do or that you're living a lifestyle that you aren't. There's a whole world of memes about this phenomenon: people taking pictures of cars that aren't theirs, with a caption that makes you think they've just walked out of the show-room. Celebrities do this . . . a lot. So when you see them posting photos of swag in exotic locales, it doesn't mean that they are actually the owner of that possession. They post watches, jewelry, and shoes that don't even actually belong to them.

We all saw what happened to Shad Moss, aka Bow Wow, my favor-ite kiddie rapper turned *CSI* actor and *Growing Up Hip Hop* reality star. He got caught stunting on the 'gram when he took a picture of a private jet and posted it on social media with the caption "Travel day. NYC press run Lets goooo." Nothing unusual there. Celebs are always posting pictures of themselves taking off in their private jets. There was only one problem this time: Shortly after Bow Wow posted that picture, someone spotted him on a commercial flight, flying coach just like the rest of us. They snapped a picture, posted it online, and just like that, his rich boy baller image was shattered. The internet went in. It was discovered that the image of the jet was actu-ally a stock photo from a private jet company website. From there, a hilarious new meme was born: The Bow Wow Challenge. Suddenly thousands of people were Photoshopping themselves into pictures of expensive material items and luxurious spaces and posting them next to pictures of what they were really doing instead.

Jokes aside, the point is powerful: It's our own shame that causes this vicious cycle of pretending, comparing ourselves to what others are pretending, and then pretending some more.

But why? Why do we care so much about the shoulds, and why does it seem like no matter where we fall on the financial spectrum, none of us feel as if we have enough? Why do we think what we think and feel what we feel about money?

QUESTION 1: What is the story?

Whether we want to admit it or not, capitalism is our national religion. As Americans, we follow the money, chase it, and honor it. We believe very deeply in what it can do for our lives.

Historian Yuval Noah Harari speaks about this beautifully in his classic book, *Sapiens: A Brief History of Humankind*. He claims that while every other religion is hard to follow, capitalism, or consumerism, is the first one that is not. For other religions the prerequisite for paradise is hard, moral work, work that is often impossible to do all the time: avoid anger, deny selfish cravings, be tolerant, and love unconditionally. The religion of capitalism, or consumerism, on the other hand, promises paradise on one condition only: that the rich remain greedy and spend their time making more money, and that everyone else lets their cravings and passions run wild, buying more and more of what the rich are trying to sell us. Harari writes, "This [capitalism] is the first religion in history whose followers actually do what they are asked to do." And how do we know that this religion actually works? How do we know that paradise is real? "We've seen it on television."

How true that is. Paradise is on Bravo, E!, and MTV. It's on our Facebook and Snapchat. It's sold to us in movies where twenty-four-year-olds have NYC apartments that in the real world would cost $2.4 million, and in YouTube videos where motivational coaches tell us that we can have our first million in six months if we follow these five steps.

And in the process of all of that consuming, we consume some pretty clear stories about money.

You can never have enough. Enough will never be enough.

There aren't enough resources for everyone, and in order for some to have, others must have not.

The greedy always win.

Some people deserve to have money and nice things and some people don't.

Wealth is the ultimate sign of success. Everyone should want to be rich.

Everyone can be rich. If you work hard and are smart enough, you can achieve wealth.

Money matters more than anything else. Or, put another way, if you don't have money, nothing else matters.

There is no problem that money can't solve.

Money equals power.

Money can buy anything, including happiness.

LB's father always says, "Capitalism eats its young." He means that the core conundrum of capitalism, despite all of its benefits, is that it has an insatiable hunger. The need for more is a never-ending cycle, and that longing informs everything we do.

QUESTION 2: Does this story serve my values and me?

In today's world, money embodies three very important values. First, it has an *economic value*: its purchasing power; what you can use your money to buy. Second, it has a *social value*: based on what you have, money implies where you stand in relation to everyone else—your status, class, privilege. End of story. And third, it has a *psychological and emotional value.* This concept refers to how money makes us *feel* and gets to the heart of the choices we make based on those feelings. Money can be an indicator of *your* value. Your self-worth. We believe that how much money we have is a reflection of our competence, our capabilities, and our intelligence. That last one is the most powerful and dangerous story of all.

This is why we place so much trust in the wealthy. Society telling us that if you are rich, you are better—somehow smarter, more virtuous—is the only possible explanation for why we take life advice from celebrities who have no qualifications other than wealth. Steve Harvey, a three-times married man, is an expert in relationships? Gwyneth Paltrow is an expert in alternative health and beauty? Whoever *Forbes* says is the richest celeb of the year has won the imaginary prize of being somehow the best. Jay-Z is considered the greatest hip-hop icon not simply because of the amazing, game-changing art that he contributed to the culture, but because of his wealth. And somehow, we have awarded the highest office in the land to a buffoon who, after being given a million dollars by his father, amassed a real estate fortune despite repeated bankruptcies. If that doesn't say how blinded we are by wealth, I don't know what does.

How much money one has is the simplest and clearest way to determine who has won at life and who has lost. And we are desperately afraid to lose. If we feel like we have lost at any point and are ashamed, it's because we believe that our economic status, whatever it may be, says something about not just the circumstance that we are currently in, but who we actually are. If we don't have enough, than we must not *be* enough.

The story of money has left us neither financially prosperous nor confident enough to be our authentic selves and feel contentment in an economically unstable world.

QUESTION 3: What if I believed something else?

But what if I told you that the religion of capitalism wasn't true? And that the value of money isn't actually real?

The truth is money is actually nothing more than a *fiat symbol*. The bills and coins we carry have no inherent value at all. Money is given a value by the society that uses it. Money has purchasing power because the government says so. But if one day it was decided that we have to pay for everything with Cheerios, we would have to convert our cash into oat circles.

Society at large has decided on the economic and social value of money. Those two values you may not have much control over (unless by the time you are reading this book, our entire economy has collapsed, the dollar holds no economic value worldwide, and there has been a class revolution). But when it comes to money's psychological and emotional value—the value that determines how you personally feel about money—that is always decided on by the *individual*. We have the power to assign money whatever emotional and psychological value we want.

We have a choice. We can continue to believe the false narrative of money and wealth as indicators of our self-worth, or we can believe that this religion hasn't served us and it is time to choose again. We can buy into the system that has left so many of us struggling financially, afraid of drowning in debt, and not having much to show for our hard work. Or we can use some story smarts, opt out, and find our self-worth somewhere else. We can write a new story about money, and in this one, we can choose to be shameless.

Think about it in terms of adopting a new idea, like feng shui. Feng shui is the Chinese art of harmonizing people with their environments. Feng shui says that there are certain ways of designing spaces that reflect human energy and create more or less harmony. If someone came into my house who believed in feng shui, they could look at the way I've arranged my furniture and make a lot of assumptions about my life. Because of what they believe, they might decide that I am out of harmony or have a lack of peace or unhealthy relationships or anything else they believed they could deduce from the way my home is arranged.

But guess what? I don't really *believe* in feng shui, or arrange my house with that belief system in mind. I have not assigned the same value to the placement of my furniture that they have. Nothing more, nothing less. It doesn't mean I don't use furniture, it doesn't mean that I don't arrange it in a way that is pleasing to me, it doesn't mean that I don't really, really like my furniture. It just means that I don't believe that story and I don't place the same value on it as does that system.

The same can be true for your relationship with money. If you refuse to believe in the story that ties psychological value to money (and breeds shame, pretense, and envy), it doesn't mean that you don't need money, or that you can't use or accumulate money, or even that you can disregard advice on how to better manage your money. It just means that you choose not to assign a value to it that in all likelihood could turn you into an emotional wreck.

QUESTION 4: What can this new story look like for me?

The old Erica believed that her self-worth was tied to her finances and the appearance of material wealth. Aren't people supposed to move on *up*, like the Jeffersons? I wanted to send the message that my life was getting better all the time, and that was tied into how I brought in and how I spent money. So the new story broke me free of that—after all, the idea that my value as a human could be reduced to a dollar amount is laughable. I had a new belief system now, and if you unpack the narratives that have shaped you, ultimately realizing that you need to detangle your self-worth from your financial reality, you will have a new belief system too. But words are just words. The real challenge is to shift your mind-set and get in the habit of behaving based on your new true story. What better time for me to give this new story a whirl than in a period when I had no idea where my next check was coming from?

My journey year gave me ample opportunities to practice my new mind-set. And perhaps the biggest one came when Lifetime Bae and I got a note from our landlord that our rent would be increasing significantly. We had just decided that we were going to take the leap to move to California in the next few months. Unfortunately, neither of us had a job waiting for us, and we needed to save some money for the move, to create a cushion for when we got there. I wasn't working a regular schedule, and the consulting pipeline was running dry, so I was saving as much as I could, but the rent increase made saving seem largely impossible. It was decision time: keep pouring all of our income into rent, or do a major downsize. Right away.

The old Erica would have decided very quickly that downsizing wasn't an option. What would people think? It's not like we were living an extravagant lifestyle in the first place. How do you downsize from a one-bedroom? We were already having to move out of our first married apartment? Moving down from a one-bedroom is something that twenty-two-year-olds do, not people knocking on thirty's door.

But despite these voices in my head screaming the old story at me, I decided to be unashamed and do what needed to be done. A year and a half after getting married, LB and I moved into a single bedroom in a shared home we found on Craigslist.

The home was beautiful. The roommates, however, were . . . not. It was a true cuckoo's nest. The owner of the home was a white man for whom this was an income-only property. He didn't live there but often stopped by. The house "manager" was a single, politically conservative black male nanny who we suspected may have been involved in a secret romantic relationship with the owner of the house. Nanny was nosy and would hover over me while I cooked, cleaning behind me as I went. He once knocked on the door of the bathroom, apropos of nothing, and cheerfully reminded me not to flush my tampons because he didn't want to have to call a plumber. He also did not get along with our other housemate, a Haitian chemistry professor who sat up nights yelling on the phone with his wife, who lived in Florida.

Living there for the three months leading up to our move to California would have been bad enough. But LB suffered an injury—a torn Achilles—and had to have surgery that, with serious complications, put him out of work for six months. As a contract employee he only had a limited amount of workman's comp, and therefore, our great plan to save suddenly had another monkey wrench thrown at it. We would have to stay at least another three to four months. Despite everything I had been through, having to live in this house for longer than we'd planned could have felt like a new personal low.

But shameless Erica, the one whose new story didn't assign emotional value to her finances, said, "This situation is where I am, not who I am. I am still a talented, kind, fierce, brilliant force to be reckoned with in the world. My light has not been dimmed. And I am fly. I am dope. And I have everything I need."

Yes. I said that. Out loud. Over and over again. I became an affirmation machine. Just call me the black Louise Hay. And then I would follow it with "Money is just a tool. Not a religion, not a god, and not a ruler to measure myself with in any way. I am still absolutely *everything*."

Little by little, as I said these things, I started to believe them. I started to be unbothered by financial hardships and no longer uncomfortable stating them as inconsequential facts rather than dark secrets.

And this feeling remained true even when the tides turned and a few months later we were living in Los Angeles, driving up the coast, working for ourselves, and celebrating all of the wonderful things that were happening in my new professional life. I felt no shame a year later when I sold my first book to a major publisher and was handed a check bigger than any I'd ever received in my life. No shame in having earned something that many only dream about. No shame in enjoying a life-style that just a year ago I couldn't have imagined was possible. Just gratitude. In all financial states, I remain both grateful and shameless.

YOUR TURN

Now let me be honest: The shift from one story about money to another may take time. In a society where every advertisement and song plays on your belief that your worth is tied to your wealth, you will have to train your mind. We all have different ways of developing mind-sets and new habits: Writing out affirmations, putting Post-it notes up on your wall or reminders on your phone. Unfollowing social media accounts that make you feel bad about your income or envious of someone else's lifestyle. Deliberately creating opportunities to talk openly and honestly about your finances. Checking yourself not just when you are feeling low but also when you're feeling high, analyzing the root of your joy when you buy something. Questioning why you are posting about your possessions or your trip or the financial trappings of success. Are you proud of them, or of the work that you put in to achieving them? Are you posting because this thing makes you feel better about yourself? If so, why?

Think about giving a percentage of your income away, no matter how much you make, as a reminder that since how much you have isn't a reflection of who you are, there is no need to hoard it all for yourself. Even if you don't have much, you always have enough to share. (This is a secular version of the religious principle of tithing—setting aside 10 percent of your income, no matter how big or small it may be, for God, as a symbol of your gratitude and a recognition of the fact that ultimately, all increase comes from above anyway.)

These are all small steps that you can take to help lock this new story into your brain's muscle memory. And doing so may have a host of different outcomes. For me, it resulted in freedom from shame and anxiety that had nothing to do with my income. For you, it may help you make better decisions that lead you to more financial wealth and prosperity, or it may cause you to strip yourself of the excess that you have and live a lifestyle that isn't shaped by maintaining the perception of economic security. It may help you reject the stories that tell you that you need to have all of that money and those material possessions to be happy. It may cause you to be more confident in demanding what your work is worth in the marketplace, or it may make you more content with where you currently are, so you can finally stop chasing a dollar. It may cause you to face your fears. You might find you can open the bills that you were too afraid to open. Or be unapologetic about investing your money in yourself—whether that's in experiences or your business—rather than in things.

Whatever it does, I hope that believing a new story about money makes you shameless. I hope that it helps you make whatever decisions are right for you with less emotional attachment. I hope it makes you more aware of just how many others are wrestling with financial anxiety and insecurity just like you and that we're all in this together. And I hope that it helps you know that every ounce of you—from the top of your head to the soles of your feet, and all of the soul and life in between—is worth more than any dollar amount could ever represent.

You can bank on that.

OLD STORY: Money determines your self-worth.

TRUE STORY: Money holds whatever value
I choose to give it.

CHAPTER 8

THE STORY OF TIME

"How did it get so late so soon?"
—DR. SEUSS

I have always been a girl on the move. A woman with places to go. My motto is "early is on time, and on time is late." That philosophy guides how I show up for everything, not just appointments and events, but also life. I have always felt that whenever I arrive at a certain place—a career milestone, a relationship, even a revelation or an insight—I'm late, as if there is someone waiting at the door, looking at me with a disapproving stare that says, "Really? You're just getting here? It's over. You missed it." What the "it" is, I'm never really sure, but I somehow feel that if I had arrived sooner, I would know.

Here I was, trying to rewrite stories and build a new life with the sound of the shot clock pounding louder and louder in my head. How ridiculous and indulgent of me to be trying to figure all of this out in my *late twenties*! I should have made decisions like this much sooner. I had been on the fast track and now had jumped off. There was no way I could make up the time I was losing every day. So I had to hurry, move through each step of this process as quickly as I could.

Perhaps this obsession with time (and speed and age) started when I was a child. I remember how impressed my parents' friends were when I would read out loud from the newspaper. I wasn't just smart. I was smart *for my age*. I prided myself on being able to go places with my parents and behave maturely. No whining or interrupting from me. I was like one of the adults. Well behaved. Calm. Engaged in the conversation. My grandmother would talk to me as if I were an adult, and I heard my parents receive praise about how mature I acted. The notes on my report cards always reflected that I was advanced for my age. I was reading novels at seven years old. Directing the youth choir at eleven. I remember the look in my parents' eyes when I was the youngest winner of the school spelling bee.

Accomplishing milestones early, faster than was expected of me, became my calling card. When I transferred to a new school in the fifth grade, I found out on the first day of class that my classmates had taken Beginner's Typing the previous year. I had never touched a keyboard. I was . . . *behind*. My teacher assured me that it wouldn't be a problem. She said that if I followed along I would catch up soon enough. Well, soon enough wasn't soon enough for me. I asked my father to drop me off an hour early at school every morning so that I could log extra hours in the computer lab. I didn't want just to catch up. I wanted to pass my classmates. And soon enough, I did.

I carried the idea that speed and mastery were doubly virtuous into adulthood where, to my surprise, the world at large prized prodigious behavior as well. As I began racking up awards and accolades for my activism and political work, 75 percent of them came with a recognition of my age. I was on more "30 Under 30" lists than I can count. I was the youngest appointed member of the World Economic Forum's Global Agenda Council on Social Media, and was on *Washington Life*'s "Young & the Guest List" every year.

To this day, I wonder how much of my obsession with speed and youth influenced the very nature of my career. I built an entire career off of the idea that young people were the key to changing the world and that if everyone would just get out of the way, we could do things faster and better than what others had told us was possible. In the political world, I was known as a millennial evangelist. At twenty-four, I was running the youth outreach arm of the Center for American Progress and had a staff of people who were all my age or younger. That was the job that put me on the map and in front of the television camera. My job was to talk about the needs and role of young people in everything from education reform to environmental advocacy to criminal justice. Our entire philosophy was that young people would save the world, and that we would do it right now. My responsibility was to make sure that we were included in conversations, given the proverbial seat at the table. And it was a worthwhile endeavor.

I stand by the belief that young people are a critical part of social change and should be listened to, supported, celebrated, and even followed. But what I didn't realize then was that a side effect of my youth advocacy was that it fed my own obsession with youth and the idea of limited time. What happens to a youth evangelist when they're no longer young? By the time I hit twenty-six, I felt like an old woman. What if I became one of those aging millennials who could no longer relate to youngsters? Miss one new social media platform or one pop culture trend, and suddenly you're out of touch. I needed to do as much as possible before I became irrelevant to the culture that mattered most to me. And that made me more impatient than ever.

Add into the mix my daddy's death at the age of forty-two, and I was a woman on amphetamines. His loss had imprinted on my mind the unpredictability of life. I always knew forty-two was young to die, but I never realized just how young until I became an adult. Suddenly I started evaluating everyone's age in relation to my father. Jay-Z is older than my father was? Halle Berry? Barack Obama?

While he had accomplished so much in his forty-two years, what haunted me most was that my father still had so much more that he wanted to do. He wanted to grow his church. He wanted to move into a bigger house. He wanted to travel the world. He wanted to write a book.

I was not only struck by how little time he had been given, but also by just how much more I wished I'd done while he was here. I was only sixteen when he died, yet I felt like there were so many more things I could have done to bring him joy had I known he had so little time here. My father believed so much in my talents, I felt guilty that I hadn't given him a return on his investment. He wanted me to model—maybe I could have pursued it more? He paid for piano lessons so that I could play like him, but I never took to it. Maybe I could have learned it faster? Brandy was rich and famous by sixteen. So was Beyoncé. If I had been better in some way, in some thing, couldn't that have been me, *sooner*? And while all of this might sound irrational now, when time taunts you, it's hard to give it a reality check.

Ultimately, both of those realities—my father's life being cut short before he could realize his dreams, and me not yet having done all that I wanted to do to make him proud—meant that I needed to cram as much in as fast as I could. In case I never made it to forty-two. Or in case I lost another loved one.

QUESTION 1: What is the story?

Sure, my firsthand story of loss influenced me in ways that are unique, just like the things that influence your life are unique to you. Perhaps you have come from a place where it wasn't expected that you would live past twenty-five. Or grown up in an environment where all of the women were married with children by thirty. Or perhaps you don't even know *why* you feel the way you feel. But somehow, regardless of our backgrounds, despite any and all differences, when it comes to time, most of us feel the same way: rushed. In a hurry. Disappointed at our own rate of progress. Guilty for not having done something already. Desperately clinging to the idea of youth. To be young in America is to be fresh, vibrant, beautiful, fertile, desired. Everywhere we look, youth is prized; we try to sell it, capture it, and drink it from its fountain gallons at a time. And that's because the cultural stories shout these ideas at us around the clock (no pun intended).

Society has told us that in all things, the faster the better. Speed is the ultimate indicator of how good or effective something is. A successful weight loss program is one that can guarantee results in the shortest amount of time. A reliable GPS is one that can help you avoid traffic and get somewhere quicker. Self-checkout at the grocery store is designed to get you "in and out" faster than if you had to interact with a human. Even a pregnancy test is considered "new and improved" when it can tell you the fate of your future in just two minutes—because three *plus* the insanely long five to ten seconds of actual peeing is, of course, absolutely unacceptable. How much faster can you apply eyelashes or vacuum your floor?

Efficiency, proficiency, and convenience are most often measured in increments of time. It is a powerful cultural narrative that practically handcrafts anxiety and impacts the way we make decisions, organize our lives, and judge ourselves. Consequently, we don't have the patience to wait for anything. Our attention span is shorter than ever. So we either rush and stress ourselves out to make our desires happen as fast as humanly possible, or we grow annoyed with the time it takes to see results and move on. We view wasting time as the worst thing that a person can do.

But life hasn't always been like this. Remember how I said that the stories that we believe aren't certifiably true facts of life, but rather conventions and ideas created for a particular reason? In a profit-oriented society (#capitalism), time is precious for a very specific and simple reason: time equals money. When the clock became used as a tool to synchronize labor, time became a commodity—something that, like cash and gold, could be spent, saved, or wasted. And thus began our obsession with managing it.

The writer and philosopher Aldous Huxley claimed that speed was the only experience unique to Western civilization in the twentieth century. The industrial design focus—from fast food to computer updates to car engines—was all about contracting time, turbocharging, making life and everything in it happen faster.

In the twenty-first century, we have continued that obsession with "life hacking." Borrowed from computer hacking culture, where people work to break rules and explore the creative limitations of a technological environment, "life hacking" refers to tips, tricks, and shortcuts that increase efficiency. Blogs, books, and conferences are devoted to sharing skills and tools that "optimize" every part of our lives so we can squeeze as much productivity out of every second, doing things faster and easier than before. Life hacking can teach you how to do everything from spending less time folding your clothes to finding your soul mate more quickly.

And that's because in our society, there is such a thing as expected optimal timing. Expected optimal timing is exactly what it sounds like: optimal moments for milestones and accomplishments that one is expected to achieve.

In our culture, messages about expected optimal timing are everywhere. From motivational literature to commercials, the message is: Don't miss your shot. Seize the day! Don't let opportunity pass you by. You have one window, one Eminem "Lose Yourself"-style moment, and if you blink or are in the wrong place at the wrong time, you could miss it.

What's more, there are plenty of items on the checklist of life that you're supposed to do at a certain age or by a certain age. This narrative suggests that there is just a small window of time that you have to ensure financial security, marriage, or having kids. Dig your heels in and achieve, do not go gentle into the dying of the light. Because time is slipping away. It's now or never.

This story is easy to believe because we live in a culture that believes in linear time. "What do you mean 'believes in linear time,' Erica? Time is time, right?" Wrong. While the existence of time is universal, ways of understanding it are not. Humans have always tried to figure out ways to capture and manage life's mysteries—God, love, and yes, time.

Ancient civilizations emphasized cyclical time based on what was occurring in the natural world. The sun rises and sets each day, the seasons follow one another, the heavenly bodies revolve around us, people grow old and die, and our children continue the process. Cyclical time is not a scarce commodity. There seems always to be an unlimited supply of it just around the next bend. As they say in the East, when God made time, He made plenty of it.

But the Judeo-Christian idea regarding time—the one that Western civilization has adopted—is a completely different approach. In our narrative, time is one-directional, moving forward, with a future that is fundamentally different from what came before it. God created a beginning and a march toward a finite ending. And so no two minutes are alike. This second that I'm living in is unequivocally different, and hopefully better, from the one that just passed. I'll never replicate it or repeat it. And the one that is to come leads me closer to death.

A natural consequence of this framework, then, is a preoccupation with the past, missed moments, lost opportunities, and the belief that we can somehow bend the future toward our will. We see time passing without decisions being made or actions performed as having been "wasted."

And from this idea comes perhaps the most haunting story of all, the story that sings three powerful little words in our ears: *It's too late.*

There's something we should have done earlier. Something we should have done *then*.

It's too late to change majors.

It's too late to switch careers.

It's too late to find love.

It's too late to start a business.

It's too late to learn how to swim.

It's too late to lose weight.

It's too late to fix my health.

It's too late for a new life.

This admonition relies on the optimal expected timing narrative and begins quite early in life. And the crazy thing about this *it's too late* narrative is that as time goes on, you inevitably regret not doing the thing earlier, at whatever time you previously thought was too late to do it.

LB's story is a perfect example of this thinking. He is and always will be a creative. But when he realized this as a junior in college, he believed that it was too late to change his major to focus on his passion. Instead, he slogged through another two years in a major he hated. He continued to be so affected by this narrative that he was afraid to let go of his steady, well-paying day job to focus on his true calling. But despite the fact that his nine-to-five at the Department of Homeland Security was mind-numbingly boring, had no potential for growth, and was about as far outside of his interests as carpentry would have been for me, he held on to the job until he was twenty-nine years old, while doing wonderful, creative projects on the side.

When he finally allowed himself the opportunity to pursue his vision of being a full-time creative director, we knew we needed to move to LA. That's when the "it's too late" choir really turned up the volume. During the first year, he was besieged by the idea that he had wasted his twenties. He felt as if he had nothing to show for those years and that there was no way he could make them up. But the truth is, the side hustle creative work that he had done for the past decade—much of which was objectively successful—gave him more real-world experience than the people fresh out of design school he was comparing himself to.

I have been the victim of this story too. Not only had I also believed that it was too late to change my major in college (we're made for each other, I guess . . .) I had the *it's too late* blues over and over again throughout my career. I remember just a few years ago feeling as if I had missed out on my media moment by not capitalizing on the period during which I was a highly sought after commentator. When I first started doing television, there weren't that many "expert" voices on CNN and MSNBC who looked or sounded like me: African American, millennial, woman. Unfortunately, I didn't enjoy being one of those voices. I loved television, but I didn't like talking about politics, and I really didn't like the format. I hated the mad scramble to prepare to talk about topics with only fifteen minutes of prep time before going on air. I wasn't sure that I wanted to be known as a political analyst. I may have loved the mic, but I didn't love what they wanted me to say on it. Debating conservatives and talking in sound bites all day, despite my being good at it, was not how I envisioned using my voice. And so, I decided to stop. I turned down appearances, no longer prioritized being on air, and generally let punditry take a backseat to my other work. I chose to step out of the game.

But that didn't stop me from feeling envious years later, when I started to see my peers become the new "it girls" of political media.

One woman in particular was soaring above the rest; there was even talk about giving her a show. (Maybe *she* could be the next Oprah since I didn't seem to be headed that way . . .) Because the political moment was right for her voice, she was making connections, making money, and gaining recognition by sitting in the same chair that I had occupied just a few years before. All I could think was that I had missed my moment. I beat myself up, convinced that I should have just really sucked up the pundit thing and then figured out how to make it work. And now it was too late. I was not the new kid. The opportunity was gone, and I would never get it back.

The optimal timing narrative was clearly evident in my personal life as well, as it is for most women. From an early age, women are taught that there's an order: You get married and then have a baby. The unspoken, underlying biological pressure comes full circle back to the story of youth: You're not going to be young and pretty (and fertile) forever. And therein lies the constant struggle: to not see the timing of your life as wrong or behind in comparison to societal standards.

The catch about optimal expected timing in a modern world, though, is that for most things, *there is really no optimal timing*. How many times have we read the stories of J. K. Rowling not selling her first Harry Potter manuscript until she was thirty-two years old? Or actress Viola Davis winning an Academy Award and having her own TV show after decades of playing no-name characters on episodes of *Law & Order*? Or the late Anthony Bourdain not writing his first book and becoming more than an unknown kitchen cook until forty-four? There is real data telling us that generationally speaking, traditional adulthood milestones, like home ownership, marriage, and children, are happening later and later (if at all) for many of us. Or what about those for whom adulthood milestones—like working and paying bills and taking on family responsibilities—happen sooner than "recommended" because of financial realities or unfortunate circumstances? In other words, whether you're looking at people who achieve success later in life, or those who are shaking up the timetable for their own life choices in other ways, the truth is, the timetable doesn't really exist. While there are a few exceptions based simply on biology (unfortunately women's reproductive cycles haven't caught up to our lifestyles), an *expected* optimal timing no longer determines your destiny. We're racing against arbitrary times that no longer hold true in a modern world.

QUESTION 2: Does this story serve my values and me?

Here's the thing. No matter why we do it, when we try to race and beat the clock, we always, *always* lose. Lose joy. Lose peace. Lose quality. Lose self-satisfaction. Lose perspective. Why? Because we are racing against the inevitable. Time marches on whether we want it to or not.

There is always a cost to believing society's story about time. For me, the costs were obvious. Physically, the need for speed was taking its toll and, quite simply, stressing me out. I was having tension headaches, insomnia, and clenching my teeth throughout the day. As LB always tells me, your body doesn't know the difference between stress about meaningful things and stress about needing to pass someone quickly on the sidewalk. Your body processes both in the same way. I thought back to my father—the stress that his own life put on his heart, the high blood pressure—and knew that I didn't want to experience the same fate. Rushing through life was not good for my health.

And not just my physical health. Mentally, I was full of anxiety. My mind was always racing, on to the next thing, juggling fifty goals and queries and responsibilities at any given time. The multitasking, the pressure, and the lack of focus surely weren't good for my mental health. And spiritually? I was oblivious. I was missing the pleasure and joy of each miraculous moment, never slowing down to just be, to just sit in sacred presence with my heart open.

The same is likely true for any of us who are treating time as either a slave driver (pushing us to work harder than is healthy), a competitor (pushing us to compare our progress to arbitrary timelines), or a boogeyman (chasing us with the reminder that it's all almost over). These stories have made us impatient, frustrated, and insecure. So let's rewrite them.

QUESTION 3: What if I believed something else?

My aha moment finally came, as cliché as this may sound, during a yoga class (which is strange because I am not a yogi—I can barely touch my toes). This wasn't just any yoga class, but a Bikram yoga class: ninety minutes, 105-degree heat, one rule: No matter what happens, no matter how you feel, stay in the room. Three minutes into the class, I was ready to leave. I was struggling with the poses, wiping buckets of sweat off my face every two seconds, and fighting to breathe. I wanted to pass out. Then I would look around and see people with perfect form; long, lean bodies with small bones, minimal cellulite, and what seemed to be rubber bands for connective tissue. Their legs were above their heads. Their arms were wrapped around their backs. They looked perfect. I looked in the mirror and saw my big, soft thighs, my barely bent back, the obvious pain and exhaustion on my face, and could think about nothing but time: *How quickly can I master this? How much longer is this class going to be? When will I be that good? When can I get out of here?* I would look at the clock every minute, wondering how much time had passed. After what felt like thirty minutes, I would check again to see that only one more minute had gone by. The more I focused on time, the more it felt like it was taunting me.

Suddenly my time-obsessed musings were broken by the instructor's voice. "Know that you're doing the best you can, in this very moment," he said. "Do not worry about tomorrow or the end of class or even the next pose. Your practice is now and that is a gift. Stay in the now. This is your best. That is all that matters."

I felt like he was speaking directly to me. In that moment, I released. I felt each muscle in my body in a new way. I felt the sweat trickling down my face but didn't rush to wipe it away. I let it drip slowly down my neck and drop to the floor. And everything was okay. I heard my labored breathing begin to slow. I didn't look at anyone else, or the clock, or even my own progress in the mirror. I locked in on my body and did the best I could. And with each pose, I felt my muscles relax a bit more. I stretched farther. I stayed in my body, and before I knew it, the class was over.

Really, all that had changed was my focus and my perspective. *I forgot about time.* As I left the studio, the instructor's statement played over and over in my head: *Stay in the now.* He was, in his own way, telling us that *this moment isn't a commodity, it's a gift.* This is your best. That's all that matters.

I realized that the best that I can do in this very moment doesn't make time pass any slower or faster. And the less that I worried about time, the deeper I was able to stretch. I can't beat time. But if I stop thinking of time as something to spend, waste, or lose, I can simply enjoy it. I finally understood that we're all doing the best we can in each moment. Life is a practice.

So, I wondered, *what if I applied that philosophy to my entire life? What if I could be so present that I could value the time I'm spending now more than the passing of time? What if I began to believe that time wasn't chasing me or racing me but was simply walking beside me. As I live, move, and breathe, time does the same: steady, calm, gifting me with the opportunity to experience every part of my life right in this moment.*

We all know that slowing down and smelling the roses is easier said than done. Especially in a society that is paying you to pick and sell those roses as fast as you possibly can. What could I do to actually create more moments that felt like in that class, as if time were standing still? You know the feeling you have during your first kiss?

When you're spending time with the people you love? When you're doing something magical? How can we maximize the moments that feel like that as a way to take our minds off the ticking clock and arbitrary societal timelines?

QUESTION 4: What can this new story look like for me?

Like most new stories, the core transformation that would impact my behavior was a mind-set shift. I had to start thinking differently about time. I started with some basics: meditation. I would take five minutes and just clear my head. I would leave space open in my calendar instead of packing my day running from one activity or meeting to another. I started to remove the deadlines for major life milestones from my vocabulary. No more "I'm going to do x by y date" or "This needs to be done in six months." All of these small changes helped me tremendously. But there was one new concept that I found to be the most powerful tool on my quest to slow down, live out my new story, and trust the timing of my life. That tool is called Flow.

In positive psychology, the concept "flow" was named by the Hungarian psychologist Mihaly Csikszentmihalyi. In his definition, flow is the mental state in which a person is fully immersed and involved in an activity. It's a state of complete absorption in something whereby the ego falls away, you aren't cognizant of space or time (some say "it flies"), and there is a natural "flow" to your actions. It's what athletes call being "in the zone." It is perfect attention.

Everyone has activities that feel this way. For me, this happens when I am interviewing someone, moderating a conversation, teaching, giving a speech, translating a difficult concept, or motivating someone with a pep talk or prayer. In those moments, I feel alive, and it's almost like an out-of-body experience. I'm not thinking about what I am doing at all, and I barely realize the passage of time. Because the concept is used mostly in peak performance coaching, a lot of the ways that people think about being in flow involve accomplishing something, activities that allow you to perform to the best of your abilities. But you can also be in flow when you are experiencing utter joy or practicing self-care. For me, time seems to fly when I am reading. Or when I go on long walks.

So in my new life, I decided to practice flow. To make as much time for flow state as I absolutely could. To insert into each day, no matter how short, a time where I was engaged in something that made time fly or stand still because I was putting my whole self into it. Whatever it is exactly, I have found that the more time I spend in flow or flow-like states, the less likely it is that I will be preoccupied with time.

Today, I walk through the world trying my best to reject society's narratives about time every chance I get. I reject the idea that physical youth is our supreme state. I reject that I must hack my way to an end result and that time is a marker of success. I am less susceptible to marketing that aims to sell me something the one benefit of which is "fast" or "young." I refuse to believe that speed is a virtue, and I resist the idea that I am meant to be going as fast as possible.

In my new story, *the gift of time matters more than the passing of time*. And with that, we can savor each moment. The timing of your life—how fast or slow you reach certain outcomes—is not necessarily a reflection of your competence, your worth, or your effort. And it is, ultimately, not up to you. The one thing that we know for sure about this thing that has baffled philosophers and thinkers since the beginning of, well, time, is that we do not control it. How long it takes you to figure out everything or achieve anything is as uncontrollable as the weather. As cliché as it may sound, it is true: Life is about the journey, not the speed at which we travel. In our new story, we can take off our number, quiet the clock, and just run. No race required.

YOUR TURN

Exploring your relationship with time is a huge step toward freedom. Freedom from the clock that has you gripped in its arms, never feeling calm, still, or content with the way you move through the world. Ask yourself: *What would I do if time stood still?*

Finding ways to slow down and get in the flow as much as possible isn't hard. Pull out a journal and start writing down your daily activities. Pay attention to when "time stands still" in your day. What are the things that you do that make you feel most alive, that silence the ticking clock in your head? Perhaps that's doing your child's hair. Or CrossFit. Or participating in a service at a house of worship. Or maybe it's volunteering or performing one of the duties of your job. Whatever it is, prioritize including more of it in your daily life.

And say to yourself, at the end of each day, *I did the best I could. I'm exactly where I'm supposed to be.*

OLD STORY: Time is either chasing us or racing us.

TRUE STORY: Time is a gift, and I flow with it.

CHAPTER 9

THE STORY OF FAITH

I've learned over the years that the word "God" is quite polarizing. To some it is a relic of antiquated, scary ideas about a great, invisible judge in the sky. To others it sounds as silly as Santa Claus and the Tooth Fairy. But I am not one of those people. And there was no name that I spoke more often, no presence that I sought out more desperately in my journey to become someone new, to build a new life. Faith is my anchor, and without it, I am quite sure that I would have given up and sailed back to the shores of my old life long ago.

I spent the two years of this journey on my knees, crying out for guidance, for direction, for patience, for strength, for all of the things that can't be bought but are essential tools. And so I was quite surprised when during this time, the foundation of my faith itself was questioned, somehow ending up as yet another story that needed to be explored, tested, and rewritten just as deliberately as every other story in my life.

When you think about it, there is no bigger story, no older narrative, than the one that surrounds the core ideas of faith and belief. No matter where you are from, what religion you practice, or whether you claim any religion at all, we all believe in something. Love, science, karma, a political ideology, the markets . . . Belief is a trust, a confidence in what we hold to be right and true even without concrete, definitive evidence. Faith is, by definition, trust in something that can't be proven. When that belief and that faith involve a power or source greater than ourselves—God, the Divine—we call it a spiritual belief system or our personal faith. The formal institutions that guide how people practice that faith are called religion, and all three—belief, faith, and religion—have been in some way connected to every aspect of human civilization across the globe—the good, the bad, and the ugly. They have been the muse of artistic genius, the foundation of cultures and governments, the cause of war and peace, and the inspiration for the greatest scientific discoveries of our time. Humans everywhere have wrestled with the questions of what it means to be alive in relation to an unknowable, ineffable Spirit since the beginning of time.

As a pastor's kid, my story was unique, and yet underneath the skin, in the blood and bones of it all, perhaps its themes made it not quite that different from many other stories I've heard from my peers, so many of whom have a desire to believe in something, to have faith, and to practice their own spirituality in a world that has made it difficult to do so. I had to wrestle with my own faith story during this journey year because of the obvious. My father died preaching a sermon on "New Life." Clearly, there was no way for me to think about transforming my life without remembering him or the context in which he uttered his last words.

On that Sunday morning long ago, my father wasn't talking about some feel-good, motivational idea. He was quite clear on the Who, the What, and the Why of this new life that he spoke of: It was given by God, for God's glory. To him there was no new life without God. And he and my mother passed that belief on to me. Faith was the very first gift that my parents gave me. Prayers were said over me in the womb. My lullabies were hymns, and we read and declared scriptures together as a family before leaving the house and going to bed every evening. The belief system that they passed on to me was as central to our family as was love.

And that belief system was Christianity. It was my native tongue.

When I was five years old, already just as comfortable in a church pew as on a playground, I kneeled on my bedroom floor with my mother reading a Christian version of *The Three Little Pigs*. I have no idea what exactly was Christian about it (maybe the Devil was the big bad wolf?), but at the end was a child-friendly invitation to accept Jesus Christ into my heart. I looked up at my mother and said, "Mommy, can I do it?" Right then and there, I repeated after her, saying the Sinner's Prayer, and became BFFs with Jesus. He was in me. And me? *I was all in.*

But unlike a lot of my peers who grew up in the church and religious households, I took to religion like a fish to water. I loved it. I'm not exactly sure why I connected so deeply and authentically to religion when so many of my friends saw it as a burden. I chalk that up to nature just as much as nurture. You know how some people seem wired for musical talent or athletic ability? Well I was wired for faith. I am, as a person, more poetry than prose. I love drama and beautiful language and tradition of all kinds, so the rituals of worship and prayer were perfect for me. I loved all of the signs and wonders, could never get enough of that feeling that can't be explained, the feeling that overtook my body whenever I prayed, the feeling that I wasn't alone in this world.

My parents did a good job of avoiding the two most common pitfalls that make children frustrated by and skeptical of religion: general lameness and hypocrisy. My father was the epitome and arbiter of cool in my world—he didn't have a wack bone in his body. As a former youth pastor and someone forever young at heart, he kept faith fun for me. Even at sixteen, I thought he, a forty-plus-year-old man, was cooler than I was. He was more in touch with popular culture and could connect with people from all walks of life in a way that I hadn't yet learned to. He knew all the new music, new movies, new styles, and new slang, and all of my friends, even those whose lives were nothing like my own, who had experienced more of the world than I ever would, who seemed both dangerous and cool to me, looked up to *him*. With him, church could never be corny. Because I went to preppy, white schools that were far away from home, church was where I could revel in my blackness, hang out with my best friend, meet cute boys, talk about the latest movies, and listen to go-go music. (DC's unique musical gift to the world. Look it up.)

And what my father covered with coolness, my mother covered in integrity. There was no hypocrisy to be found. She was not one of those "fake" Christians. She made clear that honoring God through her actions—kindness, generosity, no gossip, forgiveness, making hard decisions to do what was right—was the most important element of her full life. There was no "Debbie" vs. "First Lady Debbie," no one way at home vs. another way at church. She was as authentic as they come, and both she and my father practiced what they preached.

Together, they taught me that the most important aspects of our religious life were having a personal relationship with God, being loving, and trying very hard to be like Christ. Sure, there were a ton of rules—celibacy until marriage, no drinking or cursing, PG movies only—but to me, they never overtook the meaning behind them. No matter how much they were emphasized, they always felt supplemental, not foundational, to our faith. And I was a Goody Two-shoes, too afraid to break any rules anyway, so the rules didn't make me feel oppressed or stifled. When I was twelve years old, my father baptized me. It was the only time that I, Ms. "I Can't Swim," was completely okay going under water. With Daddy's hands to hold me and the

Holy Spirit to fill me, I was dunked in the water and came up committed for life.

My church was small, kind of like a big extended family, and to
my knowledge there were no scandals of the kind that usually tear
churches apart. No discrepancies with finances, no sexual assault
cases. We were, very simply, a community of people who loved God,
loved one another, and, although imperfect, were trying our best
to follow God's will in the world. We fed the hungry, found shelter
for the homeless, celebrated one another's wins, loved one another
through losses, nurtured the babies, and buried the dead. We had
built our own little world that was a refuge from the chaos. I loved my
community, and with them I loved God.

This passion continued throughout college, where I joined the
black Christian groups on campus and even led my own Bible study
for a short time. I had lots of friends and was in other groups as well
(shout out to Ebony Readers Onyx Theater, the fiercest spoken word
group in North Carolina). But in all of my circles, I was the religious
friend. And so I lived, in my Christian bubble, happily ever after.

That is, until I entered the world of politics.

My first job after college was at the Leadership Conference on
Civil Rights, a national advocacy coalition on K Street, right in the
epicenter of Washington politics. Now called the Leadership Conference on Civil and Human Rights, they are a coalition that has
brought together over two hundred national civil and human rights
organizations to fight collectively for critical civil rights legislation
since 1954. If there's a major national organization working in Washington to protect the interests of a marginalized group—from the
NAACP to the National Organization for Women to the American
Association of People with Disabilities—that organization is likely
a member of the LCCHR. And so that means we worked on nearly
every progressive issue you can think of: voting rights, education,
affirmative action, criminal justice reform, reproductive rights, even

Supreme Court appointments. It was a crash course in how my values manifested in the real world.

My political beliefs have always been very simple and straightforward: I'm on the side of equality, justice, mercy, and compassion. Full stop. No equivocation. In my theology, Jesus was a brown-skinned Palestinian Jew born of a single mother and was killed by the state, so . . . that should tell you all you need to know about what I believe. His work here on earth was all about liberation and love. His mission was to replace the laws of the people in power with the values of the kingdom of God—mercy, humility, love, and grace. He said that the kingdom of God was on earth, and in the kingdom of God the last shall be first, the poor rich, the sick whole, and the least given radical love. In my mind, my faith was the faith of Dr. King and Cesar Chavez. Religion, in general, was the tool that helped Malcolm X, Gandhi, and countless other justice leaders fight the good fight on behalf of the poor and the oppressed throughout the world. So for me, there was no inherent contradiction between my faith and my politics. You fight for people to be free because that's how God created us. It's so obvious, right?

But working on the front lines of politics was the pin that popped my bubble. Soon after I started working, I learned that I shared the same religious identity in name as those who were, to my progressive colleagues, the enemy of progress. Christians on the national political stage had *quite* a brand. One that didn't appeal to my millennial sensibilities. They were caricature-like villains—hate-filled, obstructionist, and regressive. They were anti-everything— -gay, -women, and -science. From my new vantage point, they appeared closedminded and, worst of all to a nerd like me, *anti-intellectual.*

I had known before then that *some* Christians were indeed these things. And it's not like I wasn't aware of the destructive role that religion had played around the world. Any student of history knows that. But my bubble had given me cognitive dissonance from it. I simply didn't accept or identify with that legacy. We didn't talk about actual politics much in my church, so I somehow hadn't ever really had to confront the fact that millions of people who were also calling themselves Christians were actively doing things that to me, and most of my peers, were the opposite of what I believed. Worse, they were using *our* faith as the very reason for doing them.

For the first time, I saw my own ignorance. I have always been good at putting blinders on to block out things that don't serve me or align with my values, in order to just keep my head down and do what needs to be done. I guess in some ways, I had subconsciously done that with religion my entire life. I had been nurtured by the good and had been completely oblivious to the bad: just how in conflict my own values were with certain values that defined my religion externally. But now I started to see. And I started to see the subtle signs that had been staring me in my face all of these years even in my own perfect community.

I had no idea that the same people who wrote the health books that had taught me about my menstrual cycle and how babies were made were also fighting tooth and nail to end programs like Planned Parenthood and cut off reproductive health services to low-income women. I had no idea that some of the preachers I grew up watching speak about deliverance and healing on TBN were the same ones who were more excited about funding weapons and war than they were about investing in the schools in my neighborhood. For years I had joked with a man who was like a brother to me and my favorite male singing partner at church about how I suspected that he was "secretly" gay. But I said nothing when guest preachers came and prayed that people be delivered from "sexual perversion" (code language for homosexuality) or when my friend suddenly disappeared, never to return, after being outed by a deacon who saw him at a gay pride parade. And it had honestly *never occurred to me* that teaching the creation story in Sunday school could be a signal that I didn't believe in science or evolution.

Suddenly, I was ashamed. Not to love God. Not of Jesus. Not of my church. Not of the people who raised me. I was ashamed to have been so uncritical and unchallenging of this tradition that I held so dear. It was as if I heard everything with fresh ears. I began to read between the lines and to wrestle with the impact of the messages that I was now hearing loud and clear.

What does it mean for humanity to say that everyone who doesn't believe what we believe is banished to hell? What is the impact of demanding that people believe in the literal translation of a text so full of allegory and poetry? And if I don't agree with these things, *all* of them, do I not belong?

I didn't know the answers to these questions, but I knew for sure that my political allies, although colleagues, friends, and comrades in the fight for justice, were most certainly not 100 percent my tribe either. Many of them mocked prayer. They rejected faith altogether. They insulted the intelligence of those with spiritual practices of any kind. They found the concept of God to be silly and unnecessary at best, stupid and dangerous at worst. So no, those certainly couldn't be my people either.

So what was a girl to do?

I guessed I'd have to be a double agent.

I wasn't going to be *completely* different people at work and at home. I would just show varying shades of my true self in each space. I'd dim my spiritual light at work and squelch my political fire in the church. Easy enough, right?

In both places, I operated under my own don't ask, don't tell policy. At work, you could know that I didn't curse and that I loved gospel music, but if you didn't ask, I wouldn't tell you that I was actually talking to God in my office right before you walked in or that yes, I believed in miracles. I wouldn't talk about my actual beliefs, just the fact that I was a preacher's kid. At church, you could know that I was progressive and fought for human rights, but if you didn't ask, I wouldn't tell you that I'd spent the past week coordinating the marriage equality march on Washington. Or that I didn't believe in a literal translation of every word in the Bible.

Daily, I tried to hide. Soften my edges a little bit. Tried to get by in both spaces letting everyone assume whatever they wanted about who I was, what I believed, and how strongly I believed it. I existed in this spiritual chaos for years. Holding on to my childlike faith, pushing away and ignoring the ugly parts, separating my faith from my work, all the while still trying to have a rich spiritual life as best I knew how. It was draining and inauthentic, and I felt like I didn't belong anywhere.

But after I quit my job and when I was looking for the stories that would help me build a new life, I remembered my father's words: *New life comes from God.* For me, someone who had gained so much from faith over the years, there was no way that I was going to be able to transform my life without tackling once and for all the issue of what I believed and where my spirit belonged.

QUESTION 1: What is the story?

Somehow, despite all of these experiences that were unique to me, I had ended up emotionally and spiritually in the same place as many of my peers. Feeling alone. With no spiritual home. No community that understood me. Some people who felt like this had been hurt by religious institutions and refused to return. Others simply outgrew those institutions. And many, many others had never grown up in one at all. For some, religion had never been more than a cultural identifier. Others never really took to the idea at all. Perhaps you fit in one of these categories, and my life of internal religious conflict seems foreign to you.

But no matter the specific origin story, over 70 percent of millennials still somehow find ourselves in a category called the "nones." Data shows that by and large, we don't feel as if there is a spiritual home or religious institution for us. According to the Pew Research Center, more than a third of Americans between eighteen and thirty-five are unaffiliated: When asked on a survey which religious identity they hold, they say none of the above. We are the least religious generation in American history. Yet two-thirds of the nones respond in the same survey saying that they believe in God, or a universal spirit, and one in five actually pray every day.

The glimpses of this desire for spiritual connection show up where you least expect it. The rise of artists like Chance the Rapper and Justin Bieber, as well as champion athletes like Steph Curry and Kevin Durant, all of whom have talked openly about their faith journeys, has carved a space in mainstream popular culture to acknowledge just how important our beliefs are—even religious ones—in shaping our life's story.

So it's not that our generation has rejected all spirituality, or even all concept of religion. The research simply says that millennials feel like they haven't found a place where they belong spiritually, a community and a practice that feels right. And that was 100 percent how I felt.

A project out of Harvard Divinity School, led by my dear friends Casper ter Kuile and Angie Thurston, called "How We Gather" studied where and how millennials find spiritual safety and formation. They found that some, despite this feeling of spiritual homelessness, continue to participate in religious institutions anyway, honoring tradition and cultural ties, trying to find their way from the inside. Others abandon these institutions altogether, leading to what the religions themselves call the "crisis" of declining millennial membership. Those who have abandoned traditional religion are trying to find their way and build a faith practice any way they can. Yoga studios. Book clubs. Annual self-help conferences. Even CrossFit and SoulCycle—approaching any endeavor they can with a spiritual fanaticism. And most—whether within religious institutions or without—aren't just searching for a spiritual practice that makes them feel whole, they are searching for a community to experience spirituality together with others.

But why? What was the big story that had left so many of us isolated wanderers? What was the story that brought us all, from our different backgrounds, cultures, and faith stories to the same exact place?

The Cultural Story

Each religion has its own history. Where, when, and how it originated, how it grew and spread. Most—from Islam to Judaism to Christianity—have a story of at one point or another, somewhere in the world, being used as a tool of empire to amass power or oppress others, and all have at some point, somewhere in the world, been intertwined with the state or a society's way of governing itself. Each has influenced and been influenced by politics and popular culture, and all of that history explains so much of how *each* religion became what it is today. This I already knew.

But beyond the history of religion, and each religion in particular, I wanted to know the bigger story of belief. What narrative idea had shaped our collective understanding of faith itself? What story told us what it meant to believe at all?

Well, if I boil it down to the basics, one of the functions of religion is to provide answers to life's big questions. *What happens when I die? Why am I here? How did the universe begin?* Spirituality is all about seeking answers. And my guess is that somehow, as the world became more uncertain and humans longed to hold on to something sure, something true, the idea of faith as something that *we believe* morphed into faith as something that *we know.* A sort of certainty.

That was the cultural story that many of us had consumed for most of our lives. To have faith is to have certainty, not just about the mysteries of the universe but also about how we are to think, walk, talk, worship, vote, and love. In this story, to believe in something is to know beyond a shadow of a doubt what is right and what is wrong, what is real and what is unreal. What is good and what is bad. How the mysteries of life and the world work, definitively. The story goes: The more things that you are certain about, the greater your faith.

And this knowing, this certainty, drew lines in the sand. Those who were certain conformed to the ideas and behaviors of the group. They did the same things, condemned the same things, acted the same way . . . Those were the lines that separated the righteous from the unrighteous. The holy from the unholy. The good from the bad. And the less you conformed, the less you belonged.

For those of us who came of age in the nineties and two thousands, faith and religion had been a controversial, toxic, divisive force in society. Our country may be pluralistic, but it was quite the breeding ground for contentious debates around religion and how religion shaped public life. For most of our lives post 9/11, religion was mentioned in nearly every major political debate in the culture wars. These people believe that this is right, others don't. This religion is responsible for these bad things, and this religion is the solution. These people allow this and these people don't. And each of these groups knew for certain that what they were fighting for was the ultimate truth.

It seemed as if certainty and conformity were the golden ticket into the community of faith. The riches of spiritual tradition and collective practice were reserved for those who believed with absolute certainty and conformed to the norms of the group. If you didn't have the golden ticket, you were left out in the cold.

But certainty and conformity resist change. As millennials came of age and became more vocal about our values of openness, inclusivity, equality, and freedom, as we learned more about science and identity, many of the public narratives about our religious traditions did not similarly evolve. These stories seemed to hold to a puritanism that tried to regulate things that couldn't be proven and exclude those who didn't agree. You're not a good Christian, or Muslim or Hindu or Jew, the narratives told us. Or maybe, you are no longer a real one at all!

In response to this exclusion of so many, the nonreligious secular folks girded their loins with just as much certainty. They responded with their own equally exclusive and off-putting arrogance, a belief system that said that faith and spirituality were nonsensical. To believe in science, we were told, was to know with certainty that anything that hadn't yet been scientifically proven—or worse yet, wasn't touchable and quantifiable—was foolish.

QUESTION 2: Does this story serve my values and me?

But the problem that I had to acknowledge at this point in my life was that I was filled with more questions than answers. I didn't have certainty in many of the beliefs that were ascribed to my religion. I felt like I didn't belong. Many of the people that I have talked to since then have admitted that they feel the same. They feel like there's no place where they belong spiritually, especially if after searching they are led to answers that don't align with traditional institutions but they still desire to be a part of a community.

I was uncomfortable with the stridency of my faith tradition as I had learned it, yet just as uncomfortable with the arrogance of those who denigrated the value of faith altogether. So this story of certainty and conformity hadn't served me. Not only had it left me feeling alone, it had silenced me. I was quieting my voice everywhere because I was afraid that if I spoke up about my questions, my beliefs, what I loved but didn't understand about God and faith, I would be unwelcome.

The same is true, I've since learned, of many of my friends. Because we don't feel as if what we believe fits the existing religious models, we're hesitant to talk about religion or faith at all. We don't talk openly about our faith story. Of politics, sex, and religion—the three controversial topics that were impolite to discuss in public thirty years ago—it seems as if religion is the only one that remains so absolutely off the table.

We are afraid of offending. Afraid of sounding stupid. Afraid of being misidentified. Afraid of being judged by the religion police. Or of being judged by those who firmly reject *any* notion of spirituality. Most of all, afraid of our own uncertainty.

But that silence has consequences: If you don't talk about what you believe, what you feel, what you are longing for, how are you going to find a community of people who share your beliefs? This leaves many millennials, including me, feeling isolated. Worse, it leaves others with the impression that we are just not all that interested in God or spirituality, when that is simply not true.

QUESTION 3: What if I believed something else?

I wanted to know how could I love God, follow Christ as my ultimate role model, practice a religious life, and still question and challenge a number of its popularized tenants. I needed to be able to claim my faith, whatever the core pillars of it might be, with confidence, and not feel like an outsider. And I needed people to do it with. I needed to find my tribe.

It would have been wonderful if I could have gone on the "pray" part of the *Eat, Pray, Love* journey right then to figure this out. I would have loved to step away from everyday life and just sit and ponder ideas about God and faith in an ashram in India for three months. But unfortunately, I was also still unpacking all of my other stories, trying to build a new life, and oh yeah, trying to make money.

Fortunately, I had a side gig that I could fall back on during this time that ended up being just what the doctor ordered. For the previous five years, I had been a freelance media coach for progressive faith leaders. Yes. You read that right. For several years, I had moonlighted as a media trainer for high-profile religious leaders who were working for progressive political causes and needed to be on television. Through a program and methodology built out of Auburn Theological Seminary, it was my job to prepare them to speak to the media. If you're saying, "What? I didn't even know that was a thing," join the club. I didn't either until 2009, when I was recruited by a man who was sitting in the audience at one of my political panels. He walked up to me after the event and said, "You're a pastor's kid?" referencing something I had casually mentioned during my remarks. "Yes," I said. "And you work in progressive politics?" "Yep." "And you're a TV commentator so you have a lot of media experience?" "Um, yes." "Then I need you," he said. He went on to explain that he—an acclaimed documentary filmmaker *and* an ordained minister—had founded a program designed to give progressive faith leaders all the support they needed to be masterful on television, so that there'd no longer be a one-sided, conservative representation of religious voices on the news. He knew that there were people out there who didn't fit into the box, who were doing fabulous civil rights and social justice activism. They just needed to have their voices heard as loudly as those on the religious right. And they needed to know how to say what they wanted to say. And that's where his program came in.

He invited me to be one of the program's senior coaches, and without any hesitation, I said yes on the spot. For the next five years, I flew all around the country, coaching and conducting all-day training sessions on how to articulate messages of justice and faith clearly, powerfully, persuasively, to both political and religious audiences. It was the one way in which both of my worlds collided and I could just be . . . me. We've worked with people like Bishop Gene Robinson, the first gay Episcopal bishop; the pastor of President Obama's famous Chicago church; Sikh leaders who had been targeted for hate crimes; and so many more.

Now that I was unemployed, I could really ramp up the gigs that I had previously only had limited time to take on. I was starting to book three or four a month. I'd done the coaching work for so long that I could do it in my sleep and often unintentionally did it on autopilot, but during this period, I committed myself to being more present and listening intently. I'd listen to people of all faith backgrounds tell their stories and then work with them for six to eight hours on how to craft those stories and give them the skills to be effective spokespeople on television. The only word I could use now to describe what I got out of doing these trainings is healing. I was still a bit broken from the multiple masks I had worn for so long. But you know what they say: Only a broken heart can let the light in. Suddenly, I began to see the light. For the first time, I was listening deeply to the stories of the men and women that I was training. My eyes were opened to this whole world of people who embraced doubt, who embraced curiosity, who still claimed their religious and faith traditions even when they didn't fit the mold that certainty and exclusivity demanded.

Through this work, I met a young pastor named Ashley Harness. Ashley grew up in the Midwest, in what she lovingly calls "the little gay church on the prairie." Like me, she loved church. Unlike me, she had two moms, out lesbians in the 1980s, when homophobia was even more the cultural norm than it is today and the prejudice of the early AIDS crisis terrorized much of America. Her church was a haven where LGBT people felt welcome; a place for them to worship and be nourished spiritually. She often tells the story of a powerful banner that ran from floor to ceiling on the wall of the church that said, "The body of Christ is living with AIDS." In this environment, the same religious rituals that I grew up with had even deeper meaning. The laying on of hands was sacred because here, people were being touched who were otherwise treated like lepers, perhaps the only human touch they experienced all week. These formative experiences shaped how Ashley viewed her faith—as a tool for radical love, acceptance, and liberation—and was why in her twenties, she quit her communications job to go to divinity school and become a pastor. She was living her truth—now with her own partner and daughter—healing the world, just by being herself and claiming her faith identity at the same time.

I met men like Reverend William Barber, a hulking, charismatic, and enigmatic black Baptist preacher from North Carolina. An outspoken activist and community leader, he spoke at the 2016 Democratic National Convention, and during his remarks, the internet blew up with disbelief at how much he reminded people of Dr. King. He uses the Bible to challenge capitalism, object to war, and fight sexism and homophobia.

I met Jews like my friend Joel, who both loves Israel and also supports young activists who are standing up against oppression and injustice in Palestine. I connected with women Muslim activists, who were speaking up and speaking out and teaching, even though the stereotype of orthodox Islam forbids it. The list of people I connected with through my work at Auburn goes on and on. And all of these people were completely comfortable and accepting and welcoming of people *who had no religion at all.*

I jokingly call it the underground railroad of progressive faith. Where preachers and rabbis and imams who are young and radical and educated are pushing the boundaries of their religions. As I worked with them and trained them, I also learned from them. Each time I flew home, I would sit on the plane and jot down all of the different ideas I'd heard that I wanted to research. For the first time in my life, I didn't just secretly question or quietly rebel: I sought. I learned. I asked questions out loud. They had inspired me. These people weren't just lone hippies bringing crystals to their SoulCycle class (which, while totally fine, is not enough for me). They had robust practices, rich traditions, and sturdy houses of worship. And most of all, they had freedom. Their spirituality was full, inclusive, active. Their beliefs didn't contradict their values. They were unafraid to push back on religious dogma, but they loved their faiths so deeply. I had finally found my people.

QUESTION 4: What can this new story look like for me?

It was those experiences that helped me discover the work of the late Rabbi Abraham Joshua Heschel. And there I found my new story. Heschel was a Jewish theologian who marched with Dr. King and was quite active in the civil rights movement. In his writings, he defines religion as what humans do with the presence of the ineffable, a God so big that it defies explanation and words. Said another way, religion is simply humans' *attempt* at capturing, holding on to, and trying to maximize the presence of God in our lives. And so religion, like anything else that humans create and do, can be flawed. Really, really flawed. Especially when it tries to claim ownership of the presence of God.

That's the important distinction: The presence itself isn't religion. The presence can't be regulated or limited or ever fully understood. And, Heschel says, all that we can really do is respond to it with wonder and amazement; a sense of humble awe at that which we can't understand but can see and feel all around us. That is what our spirituality and faith should be based on.

Bingo. That was the new story that I was looking for. I needed something that didn't equate religion with belief and belief with certainty. I needed something that allowed me to question and challenge and, sometimes, just do away with all the rules and simply be in awe.

I began to think about how this story could inform my new life. What if we viewed God and belief, not with a sense of certainty, but instead with a sense of wonder? Wonder, as a noun, is a feeling of surprise and admiration caused by something beautiful and *inexplicable*. And, as a verb, it is to be curious, to question, to ponder.

What would it look like to embrace a sense of wonder as *a part* of my belief rather than as antithetical to belief? Instead of being troubled, frustrated, dismissive, or ashamed of what I believed or questioned, what if the premise of my belief in the presence of God could be all about curiosity and awe?

Personally, what if I admitted that God was a mystery and that the greatest joy of my life, the place where I found strength, was in the searching and worshipping the majesty of that which I couldn't understand? And what if, with this wonder, I still allowed myself the freedom to practice my faith with the traditions that had been passed down to me from my elders, the traditions that I loved so much?

What would happen if those who identified as religious people would recognize the limits of their religion—understand it as fallible and flawed just as humans are fallible and flawed—and therefore welcome those who didn't conform?

As I studied further, I found out that this radical story and behavior that I was suggesting wasn't actually as new or radical as it sounded. Generations ago, before religion became so institutionalized, there were people called mystics. Mystics can be found in all religious traditions, from indigenous and folk religions to the Abrahamic traditions. They were the outliers, they were still a part of the religion, but they were the ones pushing the boundaries, focusing more on the experience of faith rather than the laws and rules. Journalist Krista Tippett describes them as "spiritual rebels on the margins of established religion, pointing the tradition back towards its own untamable, countercultural, service-oriented heart."

Yes! That was what I wanted to be. I wanted a faith that was untamable, countercultural, and service oriented. And I didn't want to abandon all community to practice it. I wanted to be a rebel on the margins, pointing religion toward its true heart. I wanted to be able to proudly stand up and claim this new story order and find community with others who were looking for a new story too.

And so that's what I did. When I moved to California, I also, obviously, left my home church, the people whom I loved and who had raised me. It was time to be an adult and stand on my own. And as scary as it was to be even more alone, it was also a jolt of fresh air. My spirituality was my responsibility, and I was free to do with it whatever I wanted. I began to embrace wonder, exploring questions daily. I started to read my Bible not always as a search for answers, explanations, defenses, and arguments but instead as a chance to simply experience something sacred and find, as it says, a light for my path. I began to look at every action—every step, every song, every mundane movement that I made—as worship, not just those that happened in the confines of a church or with the right music.

I started to admit I didn't have answers. I no longer responded to tragedy with trite phrases or explanations but instead just behaved like Jesus did, offering love and healing. My goal was, quite simply, to live like Jesus. Not exactly a new idea, but in my new life, the radical story shift allowed me to be comfortable having that be the simple foundation of my spiritual practice. As my confidence grew, I started to speak about this new story. And I braced myself. I was prepared for some old school church folks to raise an eyebrow or to call me some sort of new age hippie. I was prepared for my political colleagues to open their eyes wide in disbelief at my unapologetic love of Scripture and willingness to hold so dear something that I couldn't see or prove.

But to both groups, then and now, I say "That's okay." No one can *own* a practice that humans created to honor a Spirit that can't be defined. And when you say it like that, it sounds silly to even try.

The only remaining challenge was for me to find a community. I still longed for some people to share and learn and grow with regularly. Unfortunately, this chapter doesn't wrap up with a neat little bow: I didn't find the perfect place for me. I attend a church here in LA, and while I don't know if it's my true home, the eight women that I found through their Tuesday night small groups have been a saving grace. Each week, we meet at one of our apartments and pray together, talk about our lives *and our politics*, read Scripture, and love and support one another, with no judgment or litmus tests. It's beautiful. I also am a part of a new startup church community in New York that I join virtually and am excited to see what that becomes.

My community may not look like everything that I want it to yet, and I am still on the hunt for something that will give me the same feeling that I felt as a little girl, but it is enough to remind me that the world is so much bigger than any bubble. And that once you dare to venture outside of it and walk with wonder, you will find other people who are just like you.

YOUR TURN

My story could either be so similar to yours that you're wondering how I could have known it, or so foreign to you that you're wondering how it has any relevance. But that's the beauty of narrative intelligence. Recognizing the story is always the key to change, no matter what change you're looking for or what personal experiences you bring to it. Whether you call yourself religious or spiritual, whether you identify with a particular practice or as a nonbeliever altogether, whether you're a religion junkie like me or a seeker simply looking for something that you can't yet name, the cultural story of belief has shaped you and your journey. Challenging it can free you up to embrace a new one, should you so desire. And if you do, the steps that I took are the same ones that can work for you.

First, recognize the old story. Story smarts are ultimately about beliefs, identifying the narratives that have shaped what you believe to be true about yourself and the world around you. So using them in relation to your faith and your spiritual belief system makes sense. Take the time to acknowledge where the ideas of certainty and conformity have impacted your spiritual practice. Have they silenced you? Have they forced you to adhere to things that trouble you or are against your values? Or have they caused you to turn away completely from any spirituality because you simply don't think that you fit? It's important to call the story what it is to first see what it has taken from you: your freedom to embrace a tradition, practice in community, and find spiritual fulfillment free of judgment.

Second, live in the questions. Sometimes questions, doubts, and uncertainty make us anxious. Because we are taught that certainty is ideal and are looking for facts and absolute truth to make us feel grounded, we sometimes don't know what to do with all of the questions that we have. But poet Rainer Maria Rilke said it best: "Be patient toward all that is unsolved in your heart and try to love the questions themselves, like locked rooms and like books that are now written in a very foreign tongue. Do not now seek the answers, which cannot be given you because you would not be able to live them. And the point is, to live everything. Live the questions now. Perhaps you will then gradually, without noticing it, live along some distant day into the answer." Don't be afraid to admit what you don't know, what you don't quite believe. It is the first step to finding wonder.

Third, own and embrace simplicity.

If you do step number 2 without also claiming something to believe in, you will be in much the same place you started: a bundle of anxiety and skepticism, with no practice or belief system to nurture you and support you on your new life journey. So give yourself permission to start from the very basics. Allow yourself to step outside of the cognitive and just experience the visceral. Begin with a faith that is simple and childlike. Hold on to the practices and parts of your traditions that still serve you and allow you to serve, even as you are still seeking.

Maya Angelou, a churchgoing woman and one of my all-time heroes, talks about her faith in very simple terms. She doesn't talk about dogma and doctrine. She has said that the sum total of her belief can be explained in a single revelation: "That God loves me, and it humbles me that this force, which made leaves and seas and stars and rivers, loves me. So I can do anything, and I can do it well. And that's why I am who I am, because God loves me. I'm amazed by it and I'm grateful for it."

Last, find or make community. One of the most damaging side effects of the story of certainty is that it leaves so many of us in isolation. We are left with binary ideas that we are either good or bad, welcome or unwelcome, worthy or unworthy, based on our conformity to established rules. But there is more. There is greater. Building spiritual community is hard. It requires vulnerability. It requires talking about what you think and feel and believe. It requires putting yourself out there and maybe even leaving the community where you used to practice to find one that is better suited for you.

I can't promise you that you will find a house of worship that is perfect for you. But I can promise you that you aren't alone. Go online. Instead of talking negatively about and trashing communities and faith practices that don't work for you, speak openly about what you do believe, what questions you are pondering, and what your spiritual practice looks like. Reaching out to other seekers will help you know that even if those around you don't understand or agree with your journey, others, somewhere, do. And if you can't find anyone, reach out to me. Let's build a community together.

OLD STORY: Faith is about certainty.

TRUE STORY: Faith is about wonder.

CHAPTER 10

A LOVE STORY

To hear my friends tell it, I am a character in a fairy tale love story. LB is my high school sweetheart. He transferred to my high school in our junior year, just a few weeks before my father died, but it wasn't until September of our senior year that our friendship began to bloom, quickly and colorfully, like cherry blossoms in spring.

Of course we each knew who the other was already: In our predominately white Catholic high school, all the black kids at least knew of one another. I was there on an academic scholarship; he was there on a basketball scholarship. He played point guard, friendly but a loner, skeptical of everything and everyone. I was senior class president, outgoing and social, eager to impress everything and everyone. We were opposites yet, somehow, the perfect characters for a nineties romantic comedy.

I remember our first conversation like it was yesterday. Young LB in the khaki pants, collared shirt, and black sweater of our school uniform. He came and sat down across from me at the cafeteria table on my birthday, only six days after his, and began to talk. "Wsup, Erica?" he said. I immediately recognized his accent: the way he pronounced the "Er" at the beginning of my name as "Ur" instead of "Air," the way he said "young" at the end of his sentences. The drawl. It wasn't the Baltimore accent that the few other black kids at our school had. He was from *home*. Prince George's County and DC. He was from where I lived, nearly an hour away from the school. Within a minute, he cracked a joke, I laughed hysterically, and that was it. We were inseparable friends.

I was tired of riding the bus, so when I found out he had his driver's license and drove to school from our side of town, I immediately asked if he could drive me home. If my father had still been alive, that probably would've been out of the question, but my mother was graciously willing to let me get a ride from a boy. Every day after that, LB and I rode home together.

During the basketball season, he would go to practice while I went to student government meetings. On game days, I would sing the national anthem at the beginning of the game and stay to root for him as he played. Then we'd hop in the front seat of "Earl"—his 1990 diesel Benz, with fur seats, that had belonged to his father. Earl was old, yes, but had vintage swag, and we loved him.

A few times a week we'd stop at Wendy's and get double cheeseburgers and Frostys, my absolute favorite, and on the long ride home, we'd talk. He comforted me as I continued to grieve for my father, and I encouraged him as his dreams of playing basketball at a Division 1 college slipped away. He wasn't planning on going to prom, but I convinced him and said if he did, I'd be his date. As friends, of course. We had a great time and stayed up all night in my basement—another miracle gift from my mother, letting him and our friends sleep over— laughing and looking at the stars through the patio door. After graduation, we went off to senior beach week in Ocean City with our groups of friends, and something changed while we were gone. Maybe it was the freedom of being away from the familiar, but whatever the reason, on the last night of the trip, he kissed me. (In *his* telling of the story, I kissed him. But he isn't the one writing a book, so . . .)

A few days after we got back home, I called him and suggested that we meet at Ruby Tuesday's. Over French fries and salad bar, I told him in no uncertain terms that I didn't go around making out with random boys. I had a reputation as a good girl who was going places, and so, he kind of *had* to be my boyfriend. He shrugged his shoulders and said, "Okay."

The rest is history. We were together when we went to college, me in North Carolina and him back home at community college, driving the four-and-a-half-hour ride down south to visit me every chance he got. Once he came during a terrible blizzard, against the advice of his parents, and ended up in a car accident. Six hours later, with a cracked windshield and no wipers, he arrived. Unscathed and smiling. He is a determined man.

He told me he loved me for the first time over the phone our freshman year.

When I transferred to the University of Maryland my junior year, he transferred out of community college and into UMD's Political Science program. We were classmates once again. On the weekends, we would talk about our dreams, the kids we would have, the businesses we would start together, the places we would travel. We planned our lives, and while we honestly weren't in a rush to get married, we knew that we would one day. We stayed together all through college, through our first jobs, through second jobs, through third jobs . . . through everything.

Years later, still together in our adult lives, we decided to take a Friday off of work to go to our favorite local beach, in Rehoboth, Delaware, about two hours away. We had an amazing day, and while riding home that night, I fell asleep in the car (like always). After riding for what felt like two hours, LB stopped to get gas, and I suddenly woke up. LB looked upset: he was taking me somewhere special and hadn't wanted me to wake up before we got there, but the gas tank had foiled his plans. Panicky that I would notice that we weren't actually on our way home, he grabbed a T-shirt out of the backseat and said he needed to blindfold me. After questioning him a hundred times, I finally gave in. We were always doing silly things, and he loved to scare me—so I assumed that I was in for a prank. Or maybe a surprise dessert destination. Food was always the way to my heart.

We got back on the road, and ten minutes later the car stopped. He led me, stumbling and holding his hand, into a building. I didn't smell donuts, so I knew that we weren't at the newly built Krispy Kreme factory, my greatest wish. And he was too quiet and serious to be about to scare me. So if not dessert and if not a prank, where *were* we?

He sat me down on a hard seat and told me to count to ten and then I would be allowed to take the blindfold off. I did as I was told, and as I opened my eyes, I couldn't believe what I was seeing. We were in our high school cafeteria, at the same table where we had become best friends *ten years before*. He had somehow found a way to get the school to open up just for us.

I was surrounded by candles and rose petals, and he was on one knee. He held in his hand a delicate, sparkly diamond ring, and after saying a bunch of really sweet words that I couldn't hear over the ringing in my ears, he asked if I would be his wife. I cried. And I cried and cried and cried. And, of course, I said yes. Months later, our wedding save-the-date was a picture of our prom photo: me in a beaded white gown, him in an oversized black tux. "Take Two," it said. The cuteness was and remains a bit overwhelming. And, to many, a bit nauseating. Trust me, I know.

But that has always been us. We were #relationshipgoals. You know, the couple that everyone wants to be. The couple that has found the rarest of all treasures: true love.

But the truth is, as blessed as I was, I never quite *felt* like we had reached relationship goals, yet. I wanted so desperately to live up to what other people imagined us to be: perfect. And if perfection was the goal, I, the painfully self-critical Virgo, could find a hundred reasons why we weren't there yet. We weren't enough of a power couple,

I would say. How could we be Will and Jada or Bey and Jay if we both weren't at the peak of our careers at the same time? As we got older, our spiritual lives diverged and we weren't as aligned as I, the pastor's daughter and committed church girl, believed we should be. Oh yeah, and there was more that I was keeping track of on my "we're not perfect" tally. He didn't like hanging out with my work friends all the time. We had started to bicker more than I thought was good. And so on and so forth. Despite our genuinely beautiful love *and* all outward appearances, I had an amazing knack for finding things that were, in my estimation, just not good enough.

In our relationship, I was the love doctor, and every day I gave us a new diagnosis. And most of these problems were, in my dramatic mind, potentially terminal. They needed to be fixed right away, or we wouldn't make it, I said. Every problem was cataclysmic. I bought books and read articles. I came up with activities and wrote special prayers. I lectured and nagged. My God, did I nag. All so that we could be *perfect*.

And as life and adulting got harder, so did my assessment of our relationship. During our first three years of marriage, we went through a lot of changes, changes that would put pressure on any relationship: I quit my job, we moved into one bedroom, I was trying to "find myself," and, as if that weren't enough, he ruptured his Achilles, lost his job, our insurance, and the income he needed to build his creative business on the side, thus stripping him of his passion. With all of this stress on our relationship, my need to fix/save our love from what I thought was inevitable doom reached an all-time high.

Meanwhile, as I was building my new life, I relied on his love more and more. And needed more and more of it. Day in and day out, I would try to find ways to make the love that he was giving me more perfect. But I wasn't quite sure how or what that was supposed to look like. He was—he is—the kindest, most selfless, most thoughtful, most giving, protective, respectful, honest, faithful, supportive man I know. And if that's not enough, thanks to the influence of me and

Black Twitter, he's an outspoken feminist to boot. The mere thought of him makes me smile, and while he is of course far from perfect, overall, to quote my beloved Whitney Houston, he gives good love.

So what was the problem?

I wasn't sure, but one day, in the midst of my journey, he decided that he had had enough of my constant nagging, lecturing, worrying, demanding, and "fixing."

"*Erica.* I love you," he said. "With everything that I've got. And I'm sure there are some ways that I can be a better partner. But also, I am giving you all that I have right now. My best. And I know that it's really good. Why isn't that enough for you? What else do you want?"

Now, before you go feeling all sorry for him, don't imagine him saying that with puppy dog eyes and a soft, sad piano playing in the background. This was the middle of a fight. He was pissed and exasperated and speaking at a volume that ensured my full and complete understanding.

And he had a point.

Why wasn't this love enough for me? Why was I so obsessed with making this precious thing I had perfect?

The answer was that I had consumed the same toxic stories about love that my entire generation had. And they were just as harmful to me as they are to countless others, single and coupled alike.

QUESTION 1: What is the story?

Our first encounters with love stories come from our families. As children, we learn about love's power either from an abundance of it or the absence of it. What we see and feel in our homes forms the indelible firsthand narratives that take years—and maybe some therapy—to analyze.

I was one of the lucky ones. In my home, the loudest message was pretty simple, put in writing by my father in a poem for my seventhgrade graduation. The last stanza read:

Wherever you go
Whatever you do . . . and you will "do" greatly,
Know that Love is home.
It's always there,
Easily found, always on time . . .
Your resting place,
Your refreshing zone
Your still point
Your memory lane
Your compass for the toughest storms
When it's all measured, when you start to see the world
In its true light
Remember
Love is home and home is love.

Not everyone is so lucky. The love stories of great-grandparents and grandparents, fathers and mothers, daughters and sons, go back generations and can be intertwined with secrets, silence, and pain. Many of these stories handed down to us aren't even fully understandable until adulthood, when we see the patterns repeating in our own lives.

But no matter what love was like at home, we are a generation raised by a culture teeming with intense messages. They greet us everywhere, from fairy tales and romantic comedies, to government and religious institutions, to jewelry commercials and porn. How society describes love swings from extreme to extreme: puritanical versus hedonistic, blissful versus painful. Love is used to sell everything from cereal to perfume. Name your top five favorite movies. Odds are, they all have a love story somewhere in there. It's the subject of the best music, the best poetry, and the best Instagram photos.

So what is love, exactly? Society's narrative answers that question with metaphors and clichés. Love is interchangeable with sex. Love is codependency. Love hurts. We *fall* in love instead of, as Toni Morrison writes in *Jazz*, *rising* in it.

We talk about love in terms of choosing and being chosen. We create constructs around who can love, how they can love, and then debate those constructs in the battlefield of the culture wars. We set standards around ideal love versus settling.

But if you use your narrative intelligence lens, you'll see that in all of the narratives of love lies one, single overarching "love story," and it's the same no matter who you are: *Love is hard to find, hard to keep, and easy to lose. It is precious, like a diamond. But if we can catch it, this perfect, rare gem, it is magical and can change your life.*

In this story, love is like everything else in a capitalist society: a commodity. And it's the most elusive and costly commodity imaginable. We are consumers of love, and our job is to accumulate it. Love is something to seek, to chase, to have and to hold. But because it's so rare, it is often out of our grasp. And if we are lucky enough to manage to find it, it will be perfect. Perfect love is the answer for everything, the magic wand that heals all the ailments in our lives. It can turn us from sad to happy, from lacking to fulfilled, from poor to rich, from rejected to accepted. It turns ugly ducklings into swans and hos into housewives.

Who wouldn't want to find and keep something like that?

So we look. Society has taught us that the most important love is romantic love, and that's what we spend our time searching for. We have dating apps where we swipe left to find it. We have reality shows like *The Bachelor* and *The Bachelorette*. We have professional matchmakers who get their own reality shows. We have thrice-married comedians and actors doling out relationship advice—which, I might add, is always directed toward women, because finding, nurturing, and holding on to love is somehow the woman's responsibility.

Everywhere you turn, there are lessons about love floating all around, some contradictory.

True love shouldn't hurt. But also, strong love withstands pain.

You have to work to keep love. But also, if it's too much work, it isn't right.

Your partner should complete you. But also, you have to be complete before finding a partner.

True love isn't about appearances. But also, you have to look good to find and keep it.

And then, of course, there are different rules for men and women. About infidelity, and responsibility, and expectations.

Love is elusive, we are told. Even when we have captured it, we must make it as perfect as possible because in an instant, it can disappear. We have to simultaneously keep it safe and also aggressively extract all that there is out of it. That's why we want as much of it as possible. And why wouldn't we? The story tells us that love is a diminishing resource that has magical power to make everything in our lives better.

But guess what happens when everyone is looking in the exact same way and in the same places to fulfill the exact same need? The demand becomes greater than the supply.

QUESTION 2: Does this story serve my values and me?

The bottom line is that when it comes to love, for the reasons above and many others, we believe that we aren't finding it, keeping it, nurturing it, or being satisfied by it. We are in what *Vanity Fair* once called a "dating apocalypse." Our enormous sexual freedom, facilitated just as much by valuable liberation politics as by technology driven hook-up culture, hasn't necessarily led us to better love. Or even to love at all.

Most of my friends are on this hunt. We spend our lunch dates scrolling through the latest string of their prospects, discussing their last disastrous blind date, or figuring out how to tell whether or not they have been friendzoned by their most recent crush. When I ask them what drives them on this painful and exhausting search, what it is they're running away from as they run toward this perfect love, the answer breaks my heart: loneliness. We don't talk about this loneliness, lest we sound desperate, but when I asked one of my single girlfriends to describe it, she said, "The only way I know how to explain it is to call it an ache. A constant ache."

It always amazes me how in a world of over 7 billion people, so many could be so profoundly lonely. And yet people are. A 2016 study from the General Social Survey found that loneliness is more prevalent in our generation than in previous generations and is steadily increasing. The outsized role that technology plays in facilitating connections could have something to do with it. It's harder to make deep connections with people online, the kind that lead to offline relationships, and with the ability to present false versions of ourselves online, the authenticity that's required to find and experience earth-shattering love is hard to come by.

The situation isn't helped by the culture of online bragging and unattainable yet ever-present relationship goals. The very nature of social media is one that demands a highlight reel of our lives, thereby showing the prettiest and rosiest version of our relationships possible. People then compare their love, or lack of it, to that image, creating a cycle of needing and wanting, based on the perception of what other people have, that only deepens the loneliness.

But let's say we do "find" great, healthy, amazing love. Even then, we yearn for something more perfect, more magical, more Instagram goal-worthy. As an example, I needed more selfies in which LB and I looked at each other with intense longing and love, more of us going places together, and expressing our faith in the same exact way (Oh, you don't want to watch gospel choir videos with me on YouTube?).

I wanted fewer arguments (although we had only a few to begin with), and when we had them, I wanted textbook-quality conflict resolution. I wanted us to be and look perfect.

And even when it does look perfect, we're constantly afraid of losing it. If Beyoncé and Jay-Z were relationship ideals, our collective hope was shattered when they each revealed the challenges in their marriage to the whole world, right in their songs. The infidelity, the selfishness. With Bey's honesty, Jay became the most hated man in America. Just another confirmation of our worst fears; even *that* love could break at any time.

As for me, this idea of love fragility and scarcity made me somewhat of a love hoarder. You know, like those people you see on TV whose houses are packed with every single empty toilet paper roll they've used since 1972. And a cat. There's always a cat. Well, that was me when it came to love. Not only did I have a wonderful romantic relationship, my life was full of all kinds of love. I was surrounded by family and community that nurtured and cared for me unconditionally. I had a sister who I always said was basically just my heartbeat walking around in a much prettier body. And as the family's first baby, I'd had the full attention of my grandparents, aunts, and uncles since the moment I was born. I was love-spoiled.

And what was I doing with all of this love? Had I become a saint, giving away my excess love to those around the world—or even in my extended circle—who were in need? No. Instead, I had selfishly collected it and spent a ton of time trying to save it, polish it, and make it prettier. I wanted it all to myself. It made me feel good.

And so I swallowed all the love I was given whole, and then turned around and asked for more. I had an emotional tapeworm. Never satisfied and never enough.

So what about the story is wrong? Don't we all deserve wonderful, transformative, life-giving love?

Well here's the thing. The cultural story about love isn't necessarily *wrong*. It's just . . . limited. Imbalanced. And dangerously incomplete. Any story that depends on the ideas of scarcity and perfection can't be healthy, which is why this story of love doesn't serve us. The problem with this story of longing and magic is that the thirst can never really be quenched. The story has left us all perpetually . . . lacking. We have become love-thirsty, unfulfilled people. And everything in our culture amplifies and preys upon this longing.

QUESTION 3: What if I believed something else?

Love *can* change things. It *can* be transformative. And we absolutely do deserve it. But the flaw in the story is that it positions love as a thing. A noun. Something outside of us to be received. And that's why we find ourselves in the state we're in. If love is some external perfect object that we believe is scarce and constantly out of our grasp, we never access its true power.

But here's the truth that we deserve: Love isn't scarce. And it isn't just love, *the noun*, that can change your life. The act of lov*ing*, *the verb*, can change everything too.

There is power in loving. And I mean that in two ways. First, the act of loving is, itself, powerful and transformative. Where seeking love has made us needy and desperate, powerless before this force that we can't seem to find or keep, choosing to love gives us the ability to do something magical in our lives and in the lives of those around us. But more important, we can reclaim our personal power by loving. We are suddenly proactive change agents with the power inside of us to heal our own wounds, quench our own thirst, and transform our own lives and circumstances.

I'm saying all of this in a very matter-of-fact way that makes it sound like a simple, obvious shift. As if the second LB finished his *Why isn't my love enough?* speech, I immediately understood everything. But the truth is, my immediate thought had nothing to do with power or transformation. It was simply damage control.

Uh-oh. I've been so selfish, I thought. *I need to start giving some of it back before he realizes how crazy I am and decides to rethink this whole till death do us part thing* . . . I thought about my own love-hoarding ways and my perpetual search for perfection, and saw that as a result, I had focused very little energy or attention on how I was loving him. So I made a plan: I was going to quiet the critical voice inside of me and try to focus on nothing but loving—being loving—for thirty days.

And as I did it, something weird happened. I changed. The act of loving changed me, my attitude, my disposition. By focusing on being as loving as possible to LB, I became more appreciative, more positive. My heart was even more open. I became more vulnerable, less defensive and argumentative. I became . . . happier. And, as icing on the cake, it started to change him too, in ways that I would never have predicted. He became even more patient, more thoughtful, more kind. It turns out that *loving, the action, the verb,* is the alchemy that multiplies whatever bit of love is already there.

I started to wonder: *What would happen if I walked through the world this way? What if my agenda didn't include seeking love and its siblings, validation and connection, but instead offered it every chance I got? How would that contribute to my new life journey?*

I had always thought of myself as a loving person. But now I wanted to embody that Dalai Lama kind of love that would not only make me feel good but transform people and circumstances around me. And that was going to take some effort.

QUESTION 4: What can this new story look like for me?

I believe that the easiest way to know what loving looks like is to think of the last time you felt loved. And so I began to think of the people who loved me deeply. These people became my love models.

What did they actually do to make me feel that way? What was it that
made me feel loved?

I took out a journal and started writing not why I loved them, but
what their love looked like in practice. For my sister the list looked like this:

She accepts me.

I know that I can count on her.

She understands me deeply and loves me no matter what.

She brings me joy.

She listens to me.

She is always there.

She makes me feel important.

She forgives me.

She roots for me in every situation and wants to see me do
well.

She cares.

She remembers me.

She tells me the truth.

She spends time with me.

She feels my pain.

She sees me.

I proceeded to do the same for a handful of other people who
were closest to me. My mother, my aunt Gigi, LB, and I rounded out
the list with God because, of course, what respectable person of faith

has a list of love models that doesn't include a description of Divine Love, the force that causes the waves to roll, the sun to rise, and the stars to stay suspended in the sky?

God:

Offers mercy and grace.

Ever-present.

An excellent listener.

Faithful.

Gives freedom.

Patient.

Is welcoming and accessible.

I looked at all the lists I'd made and watched for repetitions. Those repetitions of what made me feel loved were the key examples of what loving looked like, so they would be the ways that I would practice myself. I decided that for me, to love was to treat as many people as I could with gentleness and compassion. To extend grace and forgiveness. To be thoughtful. To seek opportunities to respond to people's needs. To give praise and affirmation. To listen. To give what I could, when I could.

And so I did. At the end of each day, I would ask myself, "Who were you loving toward today?" And each morning, I would wake up and try to behave that way toward more people. And just like in my relationship with LB, the results were magical. Suddenly I wasn't walking around seeking validation, attention, and love from everyone I met. I don't know exactly how, but loving heals the healer, teaches the teacher, gives to the giver. It boomerangs love right back to you. And I received back an outpouring of love so great that I didn't even know what to do with it all.

Unfortunately, despite my best efforts, I did not become the Dalai Lama. Which means I remain imperfect, as do my attempts to love. But I strive to be loving as much as I humanly can. I do my best. And not just to people who are loving to me. When we focus on the transformative power of loving, we become less preoccupied with who we think is or isn't deserving of it. I am loving, and I do not stop loving for anyone. It is who I am, regardless of who you are. Because the power is in the act.

"Now, Erica," you say. "That's kind of a dangerous precedent. Are you telling me that we need to be loving to people who are cruel to us? People who hurt us? Will loving them change them too?"

Well, the beauty of this new story is that it has another application that answers that very question: The entire journey to a new life had all along been teaching me to give better love not just to others, but to myself. Re-creating my life was about treating myself with more love, more grace, more kindness, more patience. I had to love myself enough to give myself whatever time it took for me to grow or find my purpose. I had to love myself enough to accept my natural fear. I had to love myself enough to acknowledge my value as separate from my economic status or my job.

And knowing that there is power in loving yourself helps you do as Audre Lord once instructed: "Learn to get up from the table when love is no longer being served." You are far less likely to sit around and be treated poorly when you realize that the power of love isn't in the receiving, but the giving. Abusive and toxic scenarios prevent you from loving yourself, which takes away your power. If you are living in this new story of love, that is unacceptable. Loving gives us the power to leave when we need to leave.

Ultimately, in every scenario, loving transforms us and makes us the bigger, more expansive people that we need to be to live in a harsh world and not be made small by the circumstances of life. When we can give love to the person on the road who cuts us off, to that quiet classmate or coworker, to the parent who hurt us, that's when the magic begins.

YOUR TURN
(P.S. STILL LOOKING FOR LOVE?)

Some of you are thinking, *That's wonderful, Erica. But I'm still trying to find my #LifetimeBae. You got any advice for that?* Well, kind of.

My single piece of advice is that any strategy or school of thought that purports to help you *find* or *keep* love, but doesn't advise you to put the power of loving into practice in your life first, is built on an incomplete story and isn't giving you what you deserve. For those of you out there on the journey to find the partner who lifts you up, know that it's your loving—the love you *give*—that makes you whole. Until you understand that, you won't be satisfied even when the right one comes along.

I will never be one of those people in a relationship who tells single people who want a relationship, "Oh, just stop looking for love! It'll find you!" That's condescending and unhelpful and ignores the depth of the ache. The desire for companionship is one that speaks to the very nature of who we are as humans—beings that long for connection, to be known, to be seen, and, yes, to be loved. It is coded into our DNA. And the truth is, I doubt you need more advice telling you what you are doing wrong, making you feel as if your singleness is directly tied to your identity or behavior. There are a million and one relationship advice resources in the world, and frankly, I don't feel as if I'll ever be in the position to write one. Why? Because everyone is simply doing the best he or she can trying to figure it out as we go. LB and I found each other, *not because I am more deserving than you or in any way better*. It has simply been my journey thus far.

I am beyond excited for all the love that your journey holds for you, no matter when, where, or how it surfaces. Be kind and compassionate toward yourself and others. And remember that with our new story about love, you have the secret that society's stories never gave you: We hold within us the power to create the love we wish to see, in our own lives and in the world.

OLD STORY: Love changes you.

TRUE STORY: Loving changes everything.

PART III

CHAPTER 11

NEW STORY, NEW LIFE

"To be yourself in a world that is constantly trying to make you something else is the greatest accomplishment."
—RALPH WALDO EMERSON

In my bedroom stands a six-foot-tall, three-foot-wide mirror propped up against the wall, a clear safety hazard in earthquake-prone California. It towers over the room and takes up far more space than it should. It's somewhat of a monstrosity, not just because of its size, but because, other than a tiny sliver of reflective glass running down the middle, it's covered entirely in Post-it notes. On the notes are quotes, phrases, Scriptures, and mantras that I created; words that remind me of the stories that I now believe, the stories upon which I have built my new life.

There is no fail, only do.

God isn't rushing. Why are you?

"Live the questions."—Rilke

You have everything you need.

"Without vision, people perish."—Proverbs 29:18

Stay in the flow.

". . . but some of us are brave." (This one is from the title of one of my favorite feminist anthologies, edited by Akasha Hull, Patricia Bell-Scott, and Barbara Smith.)

"Do it scared."—Scott Allan

Money comes and goes. Your greatness doesn't.

"The moment we choose to love, we begin to move towards freedom"—bell hooks

I am better than this.

Sure, I could have put them on a bulletin board above my desk, on index cards, or kept them as reminders on my phone. But they are on my mirror for a reason. I put them there so that when I see my beliefs, my new stories, I actually see myself.

IDENTITY FORMATION

When I started this journey, all I knew was that the *trappings* of my life—the job, the finances, the general disposition—didn't feel right. They were not an accurate reflection of the big, bold, creative, and untamable spirit that was inside of me, bursting with color. All I knew was that my life felt . . . gray. A muddled grayish color made of mindlessly following rules and experiencing stress and instability.

But about halfway through my journey, as I was beginning to think and do things differently, it occurred to me: This journey wasn't just about a new life. It wasn't about changing my job, or stabilizing my finances, or the way I felt about getting older, or religion. It was about creating a whole new me. I wanted to be the fierce, loving, powerful, bold, creative, spiritual, free person that I knew I could be. Creating the life that I wanted to live was really about becoming *who I wanted to be*. Or about showing the rest of the world who I felt I really was on the inside. It was all about identity.

And that makes total sense. Remember how I explained that stories actually shape not just what we do but who we are? As I was crafting these new stories, they were not only changing my perspective, they were allowing the real me to shine through and replace the culturally approved mask I was wearing.

Our identity is typically shaped by three inputs: stories from our environment and culture, stories from our family and community, and stories about assumed or predetermined expectations. These stories plant messages—sometimes subliminally, and sometimes pretty blatantly—about who others think we are and think we should be. And from these messages we come to believe certain things about who we are at our core. They carry with them labels or stereotypes, recommended behaviors and decisions, benefits and disadvantages. Some of them have to do with our external identity and how others see us (race, gender, socioeconomic status, size, etc.), and others have to do with our personality traits (if we were labeled smart or stupid in school, confident or shy, etc.).

America's foolproof way to manage its diversity is to fit everyone into boxes and categories. If you are a woman, you should be demure, ladylike, silent but strong. If you are a man, you should be a leader, good at sports, and never cry. If you are black, you should be a criminal or a welfare queen or, on the other end of the spectrum, perfect and respectable beyond reproach. If you are Asian, you are smart. A Muslim woman? An oppressed victim or a terrorist. If you are gay, you are wild and promiscuous or in the closet. If you are plus size, you better be funny. Religious? Weird and judgmental. Have big breasts? Hypersexual. Ride your bike to work? Must be a Democrat. Live in the South? You're racist.

The media shows us strong stories that match these identities with stereotypes and caricatures that send powerful messages about who society expects us to be—our potential, our capacity, what behavior is acceptable based on who we appear to be. In some cases, the data can make us believe that these stories are true or destiny-determining. And when statistics say that not many *like you* are represented in a certain field, or have achieved a certain professional benchmark, or have done anything noteworthy that defies the stereotype, the facts can seem to match the story.

THOSE BOXES CAN'T HOLD US ANY LONGER

Walt Whitman said it best: *I contain multitudes.*

I believe that every soul longs to express itself fully. In psychology, it's called *self-actualization*: to fully present to the world all of one's potential. In my faith, we call self-actualization being more like the Spirit than like the flesh; becoming the person that you were created to be and less like the one the world has tried to shape us into.

It didn't take our generation long to realize that trying to fit our diverse, complicated selves into boxes wasn't going to work. Sticking to the script wasn't logical. And it wouldn't lead us to fulfilling lives.

And so, the prepackaged stories about who we are and what we are supposed to be have entirely lost their luster for most of us. When we came of age, we immediately began pushing back on the labels. Hard. We confidently and publicly wrestle with identity and are making concerted efforts to change these stories. We constantly reject traditional stories about our external identities and push the boundaries of what society has said is possible.

Some of us have chosen to abandon some labels and boxes altogether. Sometimes, we've embraced labels intentionally to redefine them and expand what they mean. Take race and gender, for example. In recent years, there has been a media renaissance featuring people who reject the expectations of certain labels but still claim them proudly and unapologetically. The cast of *Hamilton* didn't want to be seen through colorblind eyes. They emphasized their racial identities and forced audiences to see the possibility of American history played out by brown and black actors. *Orange Is the New Black* includes a cast that proudly has a transgender actress play a role where her gender identity is part of the story, not something to be hidden or ignored.

Our "woke" generation now celebrates women directors and mathematicians, stay-at-home fathers and men wearing pink. Rappers are wearing skirts and identifying as bisexual. Words that were once commonplace to identify certain types of people are now considered curses. We are twisting and bending the lines of boxes to expand until they reach their breaking point. We are feminist and spiritual. We are Muslim women in hijabs competing in the Olympics. We are constantly shaking up what it means to be a person living with a disability or with mental health challenges, or what it means to be a person living in a dark brown body or a plus size one.

We create movements designed to push back on identity narratives that have brought us harm. When a recent spate of high-profile police killings of people of color flooded our timelines, three young women created a three-word story that would define a movement: Black Lives Matter. When society said that transgendered people were inherently perverted and dangerous, thousands of people fought back to create gender-neutral bathrooms.

Whether you understand all of the ways that modern society is redefining identity or not, our discussions of it are all a part of our generation trying to define ourselves to avoid, as Audre Lord said, "being crunched into other people's fantasies and eaten alive."

All in all, we talk a very good game that says we know who we are and that society's stories don't define us. And yet, in keeping with the pattern of contradictory expectations and realities, authenticity—being who we truly are—is somehow harder than ever. Are we confident rewriting the rules of who we were taught to be behind closed doors? In the private moments of our lives? Rejecting society's narratives *about* our identity is one thing, but do we ever stop to see how all of the other narratives we have consumed—the ones about fear and dreams and money and time and love—have actually *impacted* our identity? How many of those old stories have we internalized and allowed to shape our personalities, values, and expectations? And how do these old stories take up the space from where a new version of us could emerge?

THE FINAL STEP

I was confronted with this question one day, after I believed my new life journey was complete. I was living in Los Angeles with my new career, my brave attitude, less anxiety around money, and even a new haircut. I had sufficiently worked my way through the stories in this book enough to have a life that looked and felt radically different from the one that I'd quit almost three years before. I thought I had done what I'd set out to do. Until, one day, while sitting at a coffee shop, I read these simple words from the poet Rumi: *Tear off the mask, your face is glorious.*

My eyes immediately filled with tears. Something in me shifted. I inhaled and admitted the final truth that would seal my undoing: I had been wearing a mask. I was not yet being who I was meant to be.

The old stories hadn't just built a crooked room—a life that wasn't working for me—they had created a crooked identity. A costume that had made sure I looked and behaved like a person who matched that old life.

Because I had walked through most of my life with financial anxiety, I was cheap and stingy (masquerading as frugal).

Because I had been a big dreamer, I often had my head in the clouds.

Because I had been a love hoarder, I was selfish and not nearly as giving as my values would suggest.

Because I believed that faith was about certainty, my beliefs were shallow. I talked about religion in platitudes, never really wanting to engage beyond the surface, where my doubts might be exposed.

Because I had allowed fear to be a headwind, not a tailwind, I was reserved and cautious.

Because I believed in a path, one right direction or answer, I was controlling and rigid.

Because I was seeking validation and confirmation that I was doing life "right," I could be narcissistic, making every conversation about me and begging for feedback I so desperately needed.

The Old Erica was an anxious, controlling, fast-moving, Type A person. Always had an answer. Always cautious. Obsessed with work. Outwardly religious but spiritually dry. Poised and reserved. Even though I had changed the stories that I believed about my life and the world, *I hadn't changed the story about who I was.*

I was still behaving and speaking about myself like the Old Erica from the old life. I was still wearing the mask. But was that who I really was? Who knows how many times a week I was self-deprecating and said something like "I'm so uptight" or "You know me! I'm the scared one" to reference these old behaviors and personality traits. I was speaking negative identities into my new life.

I needed a new story about my core identity.

NEW LIFE, NEW ME

We are taught that people don't change. That once we have an established identity, that is who we are, forever and a day. We are taught that we can change our outsides all the livelong day—new body, new hair, new job, new bank account, new "look." But when it comes to our personalities, we spend so much time looking for clues to understand more about ourselves—horoscopes and Myers-Briggs personality tests—because we believe that who we are at our core is likely who we'll always be. We believe that our tendencies, patterns, and personality are set in stone from birth, never considering how they were developed in the first place.

But if who we are is created by stories, and if we change the stories—doesn't it make sense that we can change too? You know the phrase *I think therefore I am*? Well . . . yeah.

Of course the new stories will change us! And when they do, we see how who we told ourselves we were can be just as limiting as society's stories about who we are based on our external traits, like gender and appearance.

Knowing your internal identity (who you are) and your aspirational identity (who you want to be) matters so much more than understanding how your external identity is viewed in the world.

If I was honest with myself, I had to admit that the old story about who I was (or who I had to be to accommodate my old life) was still dramatically influencing my behavior.

Because I was known for being poised and professional, I continued to act reserved and distant around new people rather than immediately want to be as loving and compassionate and giving as possible (thanks to my new story about love).

Because I was known as the consummate religious person, I kept quiet all of the new ways that my faith had grown and the beliefs that I now had that fell outside of the mainstream religious box.

Because I was known as a workaholic, I didn't push back when people asked me about work before they asked about my life.

Because I had been so judgmental of myself, I was also equally as judgmental of those around me.

Because I had been constantly comparing myself to others, I was still insanely competitive.

I was still pretending to be excited and passionate about politics when in fact I avoided watching cable news like the plague.

I still responded to every question about life decisions—others' or mine—with an answer that sounded certain, even though in my heart of hearts, I was thrilled about the adventure and uncertainty of my journey.

Clearly, how I was behaving was not who I wanted to be. Maybe it was never who I was to begin with! Maybe it was just who I had become to accommodate the old stories and navigate the world as I thought was necessary.

It was time to take off the mask. I was no longer going to be the Old Erica trying to live a new life. I was going to be New Erica. With a new identity. All the time. I was going to claim, out loud, the new person that I was, even if it was different from who society said that I should be.

New Erica has no desire to follow a prescribed rulebook. New Erica isn't nearly as competitive because she no longer views her progress in comparison to someone else's. New Erica loves God so fiercely that she won't allow tradition to restrict her quest to experience Him. Judgment? Gone.

I am exceedingly compassionate and extend grace wherever I can. I'm the person who is living so much in the flow that I refuse to miss a minute of life by rushing through it. I am adventurous and willing to do uncomfortable new things with bravery. And I am more confident and relaxed about my future because I know that purpose and vision guide me.

See me without the mask. Aren't I glorious?

Aren't you?

EMBRACING YOUR NEW IDENTITY

Freedom is the ability to let who you really are loose in the world. You aren't free if you are still thinking of yourself, and presenting yourself, in the identity that society's stories shaped without your consent.

The final step of your story smart, new life journey is the one that allows you to see if you are really free: *Embracing the ultimate story about who you are.* If you're doing the work to recognize and reject cultural stories that haven't served you, it's now time to reflect how that is changing your identity. Has it made you speak differently? Think differently? Perhaps your new story has brought you to a new set of friends or new tastes. Maybe it has changed your values, and you are seeing what actually matters to you. Hopefully it has changed some of your default behaviors and habits. The next question is: Do you see yourself as a new person? Do others?

To answer this question, I use what I call the eulogy test. I ask myself what I think others might say about me if I died tomorrow. And I answer, honestly, not about my accomplishments or achievements, but about my identity. Who would they say that I am? What and who has my life proven me to be? Every now and then, I'll even ask a few people who are close to me and whom I can trust to be honest, to tell me exactly how they see me. Now, this is the important part: The purpose of this exercise *isn't to see if you like what is said*. If we are being honest with ourselves, no one likes every single part of his or her personality, because no one is perfect. The test is to see if the answer *rings true*. Are you showing the world the you that you know is there, that has resulted from your awareness of the stories and forces that are trying to shape you? Or are you still hiding behind the mask?

If you are really free, you have reached the ultimate sign of your narrative intelligence: being able to recognize the stories that are shaping your identity, your very being, and deciding that you are confident enough to share a new and improved you with the world. This isn't about self-improvement. I'm not telling you how to "be a better person." I'm simply warning you that being a better person is a common side effect of the new life journey. It is almost impossible to recognize society's narratives about fear, dreams, work, money, time, faith, and love, and come out the exact same person. I am encouraging you to be okay with that . . . even if others aren't.

It's totally normal to have fears around how others will accept the new you. I worried about that quite a bit, and it was one of the reasons that I still wore the mask. *Will they question me? Hate on me? Not believe me? Will they feel like I no longer fit with them? Will they mock me and think that I am somehow a fake?*

So what if they do.

Who cares.

Who cares.

Who cares.

To quote Jay-Z, *Ery'body look at you strange, say you changed. Like you work that hard to stay the same?* You didn't go through all of this work to fundamentally change how you look at the world just to hide who you are. On the contrary, you changed your life so that the absolute best you could thrive. You have committed to seeing the world differently, so embrace your new life, your new you.

Story smarts aren't just about external changes. They're about feeling more centered and a little less crazy as you try to stand up and be yourself in this world. I could tell you about all sorts of celebrities or extraordinary people who turned their lives around, but who really cares about them? Make your new story all about you.

AND YOU?

"Rome is built on ruins and is quite breathtaking;
what makes you think you can't be, too?"
—UNKNOWN

Perhaps you are looking to change everything about your current circumstances. Or you want to find peace in a particular area like your anxiety around money. Or maybe you picked up this book just because you want to be able to have an impact on the state of our world. No matter what your goal is, the first step to living a life with story smarts is to *do something.*

Take a step. Ask yourself, *What one thing would I do right now if I was brave? If I pursued my purpose? If I embraced simplicity and uncertainty in my spiritual life? If I knew that work was more valuable than a job? If I stopped believing that time is a commodity and that money determines my worth? If I put as much effort into the action of love as I do into searching for the feeling of love? What one thing would I do, right now, if I knew that society's stories are changeable and that I have the power to write and live new ones?*

Look, I know change is hard. You have believed these stories for your entire life. And they are all around you. In some cases, as with money, entire global systems have been set up to reinforce the old story.

How can you possibly change? What if even after reading through this book, the outside of your life is still messy? (Which it may very well be since no changes happen overnight.) What do you do in the chaos?

Well, you do what Vedran Smailovic did. Smailovic was a cellist in the Sarajevo Opera. In 1992, Sarajevo was ground zero for the Bosnian War. Life in the city was brutal and dangerous, each day bringing with it bombs and bloodshed. By May, people in the city were simply going through the motions—trying to make some semblance of a daily life in the midst of terror and chaos. On May 27, a mortar shell dropped on a line of people standing at a bakery. Twenty-two people were killed waiting for bread.

Smailovic lived close to the bakery. His heart ached and he wished he could help, but he didn't know what to do. As most people feel when their world is crumbling, he knew that he didn't have the power to stop it. But he couldn't just go on with life as usual. So he decided to do what only he could do, be who he was, and start making change with what he knew. He took his cello to the site of the bombing, sat down, and began to play. Crowds formed, and through his art he brought joy to the city amidst the chaos.

You are here because you are called to be the cellist amidst the rubble. At some point, the violence—the destructive force—of cultural stories that once seemed light and harmless have wreaked havoc on your life and the world. At times they have cut you down, made you small, played on your emotions, made you question your self-worth, or left you feeling powerless to be who you want to be and live the life that you want to live.

You may not know how to solve all of your problems, but you want to somehow play a beautiful song. Amidst the chaos, fear, and brokenness that dangerous stories have caused in this generation, there is something inside that only you can give the world, a person that only you can be, and a life that you deserve to live.

So live it. Be it. Do it. Pick up your new stories and play.

STORY SMARTS FOR LIFE

Don't be fooled, though: Telling your story isn't a onetime gig. Being who you want to be and living an abundant life in a world that loves conformity is an ongoing process. Remember how we talked at the beginning of this journey about wayfinding? Every single day—in fact, every second of every single day—along the way, you will see the old, dangerous stories around you, encouraging you to go back to your Old Self.

Consumer culture will still try to convince you that your worth is money or that you have missed your moment: Your new job will convince you that how much you slave away is a reflection of how good of a person you are. You'll see fuzzy-feeling quotes on social media about winning or fearlessness sandwiched between pictures of people, maybe even your friends, living lives that reflect the old stories about youth and time. The political elite will try to use fear as a tool to pressure you to make certain choices and to support their ideas. A new motivational speaker will try to seduce you onto a magic path to realize your dreams in just thirty days. You may get your heart broken and want to retreat into all of the cliché advice from the covers of women's magazines. Or your big plan to move or go back to school may fall apart, and you'll find yourself back in a crappy apartment working to make ends meet. In other words, life will happen, and the old stories will be there to meet you. The world is an ongoing assault against that which makes you free and whole. Fight it.

You have to be vigilant and alert. Narrative intelligence is a competency, a lifestyle. Every moment is an opportunity to reframe and reject those old stories. But how can we when they are so subliminal and ever-present?

When I was diagnosed with ADHD, my doctor explained to me that my brain moves faster than the average person's. When I walk in the door, where other people's brains process every single action—"I am walking in the door. I now close the door. I now put my keys on the hook by the door. I take off my purse. I now kick off my shoes. Now I walk to the kitchen."—my ADHD-sped-up brain goes from "I'm walking in the door" straight to "What do I want for lunch?" in one second and completely *doesn't register* all of the steps in between. My mind is four steps ahead of my body and, as such, can't pay attention to all that is happening. That's why two hours later, I will come back and realize that I left the keys in the door, have no idea where I kicked my shoes off, and never took my purse off my body until I was in the kitchen, and that's how it ended up in the refrigerator.

In order to remedy this, I had to work to increase my awareness. I needed to institute habits that would help me pay attention to my thoughts and what was happening around me. And that is what we all need to do when it comes to circumventing these old stories. In order to move through the world with story smarts—alert and vigilant, paying attention to the stories that are around us and to our responses— we must institute habits that help. I call them my "rituals of resistance."

10 Rituals of Resistance

1. Look for the old stories. Stories are hidden in every commercial, conversation, movie, and social media post. And they hide particularly well in your own thought patterns. It's your job to find them. Make it a game. Like the book *Where's Waldo?* Where do you see the old stories? Start to consciously evaluate your conversations and the media that you consume and see if you can find cultural narratives and myths inside of them.

2. If you see something, say something. You can't change what you don't acknowledge. When you recognize unhelpful stories rearing their ugly head, call them out. And be specific. Identify what the actual story is that you are seeing or hearing. Most times, you'll be able to name several.

3. Question everything. Sometimes abstract, invisible things are hard to unpack. So ask yourself questions: *What is this person, place, experience, or thing telling me? In order for this to be true, what else has to be true? Do I believe that?*

4. Research. When confronted with ideas that don't feel right, head right over to Google, or Siri, or whatever search engine rocks your world. Research its origin. Where did it come from? What experiences motivated this person to say this thing? Sometimes identifying the source of a story makes it easier for you to reject it.

5. Unfollow the unhelpful. I mean this not only in the social media sense, but also in the more metaphorical sense: Stop following the lives, ideas, and output from sources that constantly promote unhelpful stories. If there are people or outlets that drag you back into the crooked room and make you question what you now know to be true, limit your exposure to them as best you can. I know this is difficult if they happen to be your family or colleagues—people or places that you can't avoid—but even then, don't be afraid to institute boundaries that give them limited access to your emotions and limited power in your thoughts.

6. Take inventory. Life gets busy, and it's hard to keep your mindset in check. So every now and then, maybe once a month, sit down and evaluate the seven areas of your life outlined here and see if your emotions and actions have lined up with the new stories. If not, it's the perfect chance to explore why not.

7. Affirm. Speech is a powerful way to help lock in new mind-sets and make the intangible more tangible. It sounds very hippy dippy to believe that words create realities, but at the very least, saying things out loud makes a difference in how you feel and what you focus on. So say what you believe as often as you need to. The Post-it notes on my mirror help me. But you can write out your own statements. Or highlight and read aloud quotes from this book that really speak to you.

8. Find community. We can't change the world alone. So try to find and connect with people who believe your new stories. Join groups online and spend more time with friends who are rejecting mainstream cultural narratives. Or start a group of your own!

9. Nurture the new. Consume content that reinforces new stories and makes you more informed on the damaging stories that surround us. Read things that question and provide context for the realities of your life and seek out material that nurtures what you now believe.

10. Testify. My absolute favorite ritual. Just as I loved Testimony Sunday in church growing up, the part of the service where people take the mic and share stories of blessings and good news, so too do I love telling everyone I know about the changes that have come from my new stories. Spread the word. Speak about what you believe, speak about the new stories, speak about the new life and the stories that built it. Speak on it every chance you get. This is the ultimate act of resistance.

CHAPTER 12

CHANGE THE STORY, CHANGE THE WORLD

"If you think we can't change the world,
it just means you're not one of those that will."
—JACQUE FRESCO

The Cellist of Sarajevo's story that I shared earlier didn't end with him playing at the bakery site. Smailovic began to go to other sites as the siege on his country continued. He played in abandoned buildings and other places where shells and bombs had caused destruction. Every day he would sit amidst the rubble and play new songs, confidently and beautifully. Eventually other musicians were inspired to create tributes. Yo-Yo Ma once played a piece composed just for Smailovic, and a children's book was written about the cellist.

Similarly, your new identity and your new life is a song of inspiration, a clarion call for everyone still living in the crooked rooms and in the rubble of their old stories.

As you move forward on your own unique journey, do so with a sense of the collective in mind, telling new stories about who we are, about what's possible, about the lies that have shaped our communities and the truth that can set us free. That is how we make your new story and my new story *our* new story. Pick up your instrument and play.

That is how we change the world.

And isn't that what we ultimately all want? To leave a mark on the world? To make it better? To fix some of the societal ills that break our hearts when we actually take the time to see them?

I know I do. The world is the context in which all of these stories—the old and new ones, the helpful and unhelpful alike— have the greatest impact on our lives and the lives of those around us. And this is where most personal development and self-help falls short. It's always all about the self. We're told that sure, all the positive changes that we make in our own lives can somehow change the world, but rarely does anyone explain how.

Well that's not good enough for me. I have devoted my life to social change and am constantly evaluating how shifts in my mindset and awareness can make me not just a better human but a better part of a community. I do believe that if we are each better, smarter people, happier people, the world will gradually get better. But to see radical, swift changes, we're going to have to actively apply every lesson we learn to issues, causes, and people beyond ourselves. I think deeply about the impact that narrative intelligence can have when we look up from our own lives and start trying to make the lives of others better.

I'd like to share my thoughts on how each of the themes we've covered in this book and in our personal lives can pertain to our work to change the world. I don't know your politics, but by now, you certainly know some of mine. But no matter where you fall on the political spectrum, I encourage you to wrestle with these ideas. The work of changing the world isn't easy—it is much more than a slogan and will require the same kind of commitment to new stories that hopefully you are committed to for yourself. Here are just a few ideas that I hope can help.

A BRAVE NEW WORLD

A few years ago, the Case Foundation underwent a rebranding and launched a public relations campaign. The new tagline: "Be Fearless." It was meant to inspire and encourage do-gooders of all kinds, especially the ones that were asking them for money, to be more fearless in their efforts to change the world.

The underlying message was admirable: To do the most good, you need to be entrepreneurial, take risks, and not be afraid of failure. In short, have no fear. But with the way the world has changed since the launch of the campaign, I can't help but shake my head at the irony of this statement. The world has always been a scary place, but now our cup of fear legitimately runs over. The threat of losing health care, being targeted for a hate crime, winding up a victim of all too frequent mass shootings, poisonous drinking water, police violence, global warming, even being tweeted at by the President of the United States . . . These are all real events, and it's highly rational to be afraid of them. If we are "fearless" now, are we being either too blind to see, too oblivious to notice, too delusional to understand, or too privileged to care about the terrifying chaos that exists all around us? Even for the most optimistic, being fearless just isn't an option.

History teaches us that the more afraid we are as a society, the more vulnerable we are. It's in times like these that fear can most easily be used as a tool to manipulate, control, and have us do things that are against our values and that we otherwise wouldn't do. Some of the most horrific events in human history—war, genocide—have happened when dangerous leaders use the politics of fear to encourage division and hatred.

In a *New Yorker* article entitled "The Neuroscience of Fearmongering," writer Drake Baer explained how fear is a powerful pre-conscious, pre-rational emotion that can shape your thinking regardless of how smart or well intentioned you are. When we are afraid, we are less open. We cling to old ideas. We are more self-interested than generous. We respond to uncertainty with rage. We are less critical and, at the same time, more reactionary. When using the politics of fear, politicians count on the fact that presenting people with threats to their well-being—whether true or not—will impair their decision making and cause them to respond emotionally to rhetoric.

Al Gore once said that nations succeed, fail, and define their character by the way they *cope with* fear. Not whether or not they are afraid, but how they choose to cope.

So what do we do with all this legitimate fear? We have a choice: We can allow fear to be used as a weapon to divide and suppress us. Or we can push through the fear, as much as each of us is able, and be brave.

Bravery is the best response to a scary world. And there are examples of bravery all around us. From NFL quarterback Colin Kaepernick risking his career to kneel for justice, to women all over the world risking their reputations and their careers to say #MeToo, iconic, history-making moments of bravery are making heroes among us.

But bravery doesn't just show up in dramatic, disruptive moments. In fact, for most of us, opportunities for bravery will come in the quiet of our everyday lives. At work. On the bus. At a city council meeting. At the Thanksgiving table. In the work of changing the world, each small action matters.

Bravery is admitting that you don't know the answers and being willing to listen and learn. Bravery is not just accepting but radically and publicly loving those whom others have deemed unlovable. Bravery is protecting the vulnerable. Bravery is stepping up and leading when you would rather sit down and follow. Bravery is being yourself in a world that wants you to shrink, hide, or conform. Bravery is speaking the truth when it's unpopular. Even, as the late activist Maggie Kuhn said, if your voice shakes. Bravery is having difficult conversations with those we know—our loved ones, our high school classmates, our Facebook friends. Bravery is writing and singing and laughing and loving, and dusting yourself off and trying again. Bravery is never giving up hope that our neighborhoods, our communities, and our world can be better.

Only you know what frightens you, and only you know where you can push beyond the fear and become brave in the name of your values. But here's what I do know: My personal commitment is that the scarier the world gets, the braver I will be. And I don't want to be alone. I want to live in a community of brave ones, who can hold one another, acknowledge the fear, and then wake up in the morning and do one small thing to fight and love and try another day.

We may not yet be the land of the free. But we can still truly be the home of the brave.

THE WORLD OF OUR DREAMS

One of the most iconic social movements in history, the American civil rights movement, is often associated with just four simple words: *I have a dream.*

Just as the story of "dreams as compass for the future" permeates our personal lives, the story about dreaming big is just as important to the conversation about changing the world. The most successful social change movements have inspired us all to dream of a future that we've never before experienced. So it is only natural for us to talk about building a better world with dreams in our view.

But there is one dream in particular that has impacted our lives and our nation above all the rest: the American Dream. I'm convinced that it is one of the most seductive, powerful, and potentially dangerous ideas in our nation's identity. Its power lies in the fact that it subtly wraps up so many ideas into one: freedom, hope, equality, and opportunity. But the genius is that, like all dreams, it is inherently aspirational and future-focused. The pursuit, the longing, the chasing is codified into the cultural DNA, with no promise of achievement or social accountability. All you have actually been promised is the freedom and opportunity to chase after your dream until you die. In other words, we are wrapping all of our values up into the idea of possibility.

The possibility of what? A house in the suburbs with a white picket fence, two kids, two cars, and a nice retirement fund? Our generation is rethinking what the quintessential American life looks like, in response to economic conditions, changing cultural norms, new family structures, demographic shifts, and different priorities. But we still focus most of our political and social efforts on pursuing it and making it something that we all have access to.

And there's the problem: Just as a focus on following your dreams in your personal life can be distracting from doing the work of your highest and best use, the same is true for us as a community. Associate Professor Anita Harris, from Monash University's School of Political and Social Inquiry, has found that the "follow your dream" mantra is not only distracting, it can also be highly misleading, resulting in people blaming themselves for failure when structural, social conditions—discrimination, unjust laws, market failures, and political realities—are the real problem. In other words, our obsession with the American Dream often prevents us from addressing the realities that make it inaccessible.

Why do we hold on to and chase the American Dream so passionately? If we dig underneath the American Dream with the same curiosity with which we examine our own individual dreams, we find two sets of motivations. One is all about achievement, accumulation of material wealth, and the individual pursuit of a desirable lifestyle. As wonderful and even ideal as those things may be, they probably aren't essential to your values. But the other theme is the idea that all people deserve happiness, justice, and a place to live a full, vibrant life in safety and peace. That is our greatest social contract.

But what about our purpose? Are we doing the work to actually manifest what the Constitution says is the highest goal of the American Experiment: "to establish justice, insure domestic tranquility, provide for the common defense, promote the general welfare, and secure the blessings of liberty to ourselves"?

Do we want the American idea simply to be about individuals having the liberty to realize their personal goals? Can we finally stop idolizing wealth as the marker of a successful life, and instead focus on a landscape overflowing with compassion, safety, and dignity for all?

As people who want to attain these basic human rights, we are in desperate need of a collective "how now?" moment.

How hard are we working to establish justice now? To promote the general welfare of all people now? To ensure peace and tranquility now?

The idea of an American Dream is not going away. And it shouldn't. There is something powerful about collective dreaming. In *Freedom Dreams*, one of my favorite books by historian Robin D. G. Kelley, he explains the value of dreams and imagination to black social movements through the twenty-first century. Whether dreaming of new social relationships, new ways of living, new attitudes, or new communities, he believes, as do I, that the map to a new world begins in the imagination. And so as we do the work, we may inadvertently create a new dream.

TIME, THE MARATHON THAT MATTERS

In the PBS documentary *James Baldwin: The Price of the Ticket*, there's a powerful moment, with the camera close up on Baldwin as his glassy but fiery eyes stare straight ahead at the interviewer, who sits off camera. He is engaged in a conversation about the civil rights struggle and the movement's aggressive demands for justice. You can hear the anger and frustration in his voice as he responds to the absurdity of being asked to wait and be patient for freedom: "You've always told me that it takes time. It's taken my father's time. My mother's time. My uncle's time. My brother's and sister's time. My niece's and nephew's time. How much time do you want . . . for your progress?"

Baldwin knew that "wait your turn," "not now," and other similar phrases were often uttered by those who benefit from the status quo that visionaries like him were trying to destroy. It is what the oppressors often say to the oppressed, what the old often say to the young, and what the fearful often say to the brave.

But history tells us that we must be impatient. We must demand what others say is too much too soon, and push beyond the status quo's pace of change. Historically speaking, only people pushing hard move change forward.

My friend Dan Choi knows this all too well. A West Point graduate with degrees in Engineering and Arabic, Dan served as a lieutenant in Iraq. He is also gay. At that time, the military followed a policy toward gay soldiers called "Don't Ask, Don't Tell." The underlying narrative of the policy basically said, "Sure, you can be gay if you want—as long as no one in the military knows. We won't ask you, but you better not tell us either."

Believing the law to be unjust and tired of hiding his identity, Dan publicly came out on *The Rachel Maddow Show* in 2009. He was immediately discharged from the U.S. Army. *For being gay.* That's when Dan began to fight back, in his own unorthodox way. Dan was loud and demanding. He wrote an open letter to President Obama that was published on CNN.com. He repeatedly handcuffed himself to the White House gates, and rather than paying a fine for that protest, he chose to defend himself in court. He went on a hunger strike. He frequently made appearances on television. He wore his uniform in gay pride parades. He was relentless because he felt that this cause was so important, and he couldn't wait.

My older Washington political colleagues at the time, many of whom had worked for progressive causes for twenty and thirty years, shook their heads at his naïveté: "He's young and arrogant." "He doesn't understand that this isn't how you make change. Things don't happen this fast."

But they were wrong. In 2010, just one year later, Don't Ask, Don't Tell was repealed and gay servicemen and -women could serve their country with pride. And guess who was right there at President Obama's signing of the repeal? Dan. Those in the know credit Dan, in part, with bringing attention to the issue that so many had worked on for so long, and with being a tipping point for making progress happen so swiftly.

That experience taught me an important lesson: Never listen to people who try to use time as an obstacle, a pacifier, or an excuse while you are busy trying to make the world a better place. It's never a bad time to push for what's right.

And yet, with all of that demanding and all of that pushing that has helped bring about change throughout history, I guarantee that most social change still happens slower than anyone involved would like. So I'd be remiss if I didn't tell you the other side of the time coin.

The same way the speed-as-a-metric-of-success story doesn't serve our personal lives, it's equally unhelpful when it comes to creating change. Just because you don't see change happen right before your eyes doesn't mean it's not happening. There is no hack for changing the world.

Changing the world is a marathon, not a sprint. In other words, no matter how hard you run toward progress, the race is a long one. And what happens to those who start a marathon at full speed? Well, I've never run one—and never, ever will—but those that have tell me that when you start out too fast, you lose steam, quickly burn out, and never make it to the end. Dan learned this the hard way. As much as he moved the LGBT movement forward, his expectations were so high and his demands for rapid change so extreme that he didn't pace himself. He went all in and literally wore himself out, and as a result, Dan was hospitalized. He had to remove himself from the fight, take time away to get better, and learn another valuable lesson that was just as important as the one I learned from him:

Changing the world—or a community, a campus, an industry, a government, a neighborhood, a society—doesn't happen overnight. To see real results in your cause, you must pace yourself and be in it for the long haul. Scripture says, "The race isn't given to the swift, but to the one who endures."

And in a world where our attention flies at the speed of light along with the headlines, we mustn't get distracted from the causes that matter to us. We have to be willing to put in the time and commitment that it takes to see results. Just because you haven't saved the Amazon, the whales, or the children in a month doesn't mean that your efforts aren't valuable. They are necessary, no matter how fast or slow the pace may seem.

I'll push as hard as I can for equality, peace, and justice now, and demand without equivocation. But I'll go to sleep every night knowing that I am committed to the journey, no matter how long it takes. If we stay the course and push with all our might, we will change the world, sooner rather than later. It just may take . . . some time.

GET TO WORK

I've spent a lot of time around two types of people in my life, and from them I have witnessed a work-related imbalance that's in desperate need of correcting if we are going to change the world.

The first are what I like to call "Professional Do-Gooders." These are people for whom some form of activism, advocacy, ministry, or community service is a full-time job. Nonprofit staffers, social workers, teachers, church volunteers, organizers, political campaigners, social entrepreneurs, people who have devoted their lives to helping others—for them, their job and their work are one and the same.

My father was one of those people. For years, I believed that he drove himself into an early grave because of how hard he worked trying to heal, empower, and love others. There was no off switch with him—his job and his work were one and the same and invaded every corner of his heart, mind, and life.

For the eight years that I earned a paycheck trying to change the world, I spent almost eighty hours a week with men and women who reminded me of him. I saw the same look in their eyes that I saw in my daddy's—a mixture of passion and constant exhaustion, a refusal to rest until every life had been saved and every victory won.

If that sounds familiar, you may be a Professional Do-Gooder. And if you are, let me remind you of an important principle in our new story: You are not your job. No matter how good it is, no matter how important, your value is not determined by how hard you work, and burning yourself out does no one any good.

I know it is hard to rest when your calling is to heal sick people, love children, fight for what's right, save the environment, take care of the homeless, or do anything else where the stakes and impact are high. But you matter just as much as the people that you are trying to help, and your responsibility isn't just to change lives: It's to live one.

On the other hand, if you spend your time working in a non-service or -social-good-focused role or industry—making money, earning a living, taking care of your family, and pursuing passions that on the surface have nothing to do with changing the world—you are what I like to call "Everyone Else." The overwhelming majority of people are "Everyone Else." You are normal. You are wonderful. You are valuable. And you are trying your best to balance the demands of living your life and, when you can, trying to stop horrible things from happening in the world. You donate to a cause, you help your neighbor, you share articles and tweets, you try to stay informed. And statistics show that you likely have a compassionate heart and a desire to do more good in the world.

From my conversations with Everyone Else, I know that you often spend a very limited amount of time *actively* trying to change the world in comparison to how much you talk or think about it. And there's a reason for that. It's not for lack of concern. Perhaps you just don't believe you have the time. Or maybe you feel as if the issues and landscape are just too complex and that you don't have the expertise or the knowledge to make an impact.

I believe that thanks to Professional Do-Gooders and the industry of social good, Everyone Else may have an incorrect perception of what changing the world actually looks like and who is equipped to do it.

So hear me and hear me good: Changing the world doesn't require a title, an organization, a grant, or a Political Science degree. It doesn't require burning yourself out, or staying on top of every breaking news development. It doesn't require forty hours a week and it certainly doesn't require a *job*.

It simply requires *work*.

Work is the effort that helps us make and find meaning. It is the effort that we give to what we deem necessary and important in our lives. And you, like all of us, have the freedom to give it wherever you like.

Don't for a second think that you do not have what it takes for your work to matter or that the work of Professional Do-Gooders is more valuable than yours. It isn't. Even they know that. That's why they spend the bulk of their time developing strategies to reach and engage *you*. The truth is, it's the Everyone Else who changes tides and makes dramatic impact. Have you ever stopped to consider the role of Everyone Else in social movements? The fight for minimum wage is being led by *actual minimum wage workers*. You know whose

voices matter most in debates about education reform? *Parents'.*
When people take to the streets to protest police brutality, it's not
full-time activists leading the way—*it's the families of victims* and
those who live in the community who are most impacted. So no matter who you are, no matter what your profession, changing the world
is work that you are qualified for.

And there are many, many ways that you can do it.

1. Work for good *at* your job. As consumers and employees, millennials are changing the job market dramatically by demanding more
from their employers, encouraging corporate social responsibility,
organizing groups within their organization, coordinating employee
fund-raising or volunteer activities. Imagine what would happen
if every single job in America included pro-social activities in the
scope of its work? You can be on the front lines of making that happen right where you are.

2. Make your skills work for change. Work that uses your skills
and brings you joy either at your job or at home can always be used
in some way for social good. Do you like to cook? Make meals for
protesters or volunteers. Do you enjoy writing? Volunteer to write
copy for a local organization. Are you tech savvy? Or a great public
speaker? Or an event planner? Or a bookkeeper? Trust me. Someone,
somewhere, can use your skills.

3. Make how you live do the work. Think of how your efforts in other
areas of your life can be reflections of your values and the causes that
you care about. How do the places that you spend your money, the
food that you eat, what you teach your children allow you to make
the change you want to see in the world? This is not about being
perfect, sounding politically correct, or performing "wokeness." It's
about working how you can, when you can.

My uncle Ronnie would often say the following when encouraging everyone to clean up after family functions or events: "If everyone does a little, no one has to do a lot." That is the balance we need to transform our world.

If the Professional Do-Gooders working overtime would do a little less and save themselves, and Everyone Else would embrace their brilliance and power to do just a little bit more, we could put out some of the fires that are burning our country down.

Wouldn't that be all in a good day's work?

MONEY: WHAT'S IT GONNA COST YOU?

I don't have the stomach to think about the world's money problems for too long because of how much they confuse, disgust, and overwhelm me. I believe that people matter more than profits. I believe that there is enough for everyone. I believe that it is better to give than to receive. I believe that if we all take less, others can have more. And I believe that you can't put a price tag on a human life. So I cannot for the life of me understand how on a planet so rich with natural resources, there are still so many without food. Or how in the "richest country in the world" so many are without shelter or adequate health care. I cannot process how children have poor-quality education or poor-quality health care simply because of their economic status or race (which then in turn influences their economic status).

The powerful sociopolitical and emotional value of money is no different from the one that we as individuals have to wrestle with every day. It screams loudly and clearly that money determines your worth. Our politics, policies, and economic philosophies knowingly and unknowingly reinforce the idea that some people have more value than others, and that money has the most value of all. And it is hard for those of us with compassion not to feel ashamed for this money story playing out at the expense of real human lives.

What's even worse is that people and systems tasked with solving these problems are often so corrupt and greedy themselves. Every day we see a new story about the undue influence that money plays in our political system. Lobbyists being paid enormous amounts of money to persuade politicians to make decisions on behalf of corporations. Politicians being easily persuaded by the promise of more campaign dollars. Others making decisions about financial regulations and investments based solely on where they can accumulate the most profit themselves.

So how do we fix the poverty and inequality that has made just getting by so hard for so many? How do we address a relentless consumerism that is destroying our environment and our economy? How do we root out the obsession with wealth and corruption in our democracy?

Wait—I hope you don't think I actually have an answer. Because if I did, I'd be having drinks with Warren Buffett right now. Many people much smarter than me—economists, philanthropists, and philosophers alike—spend their days debating those very questions. And if they don't know, I surely don't. But here's what I do know:

Shamelessness is a willingness to stand up and speak up for your money values and your new story. When we eliminate shame, we speak up. And when it comes to money, there is much to say.

It's shamelessness that will cause more women in the workplace to speak up about their own salaries and expose the gender pay gap. It's shamelessness that allows workers to stand up with dignity and demand a living wage. It's shamelessness that empowers us to challenge everyone who has a disdain for the poor or those whose elitist worldviews wreak havoc on entire communities.

And here's what else I know: When it comes to speaking up, money is one of the most powerful ways to do it in a capitalist society. It is a tool, not just to secure our own individual survival and comfort, but to show what we believe in and what we want to see for the collective. When it comes to changing the world, we must reject the idea of money as our personal value and instead adopt the idea of money as our vote.

P. T. Barnum once said that money is a terrible master but an excellent servant. So how can we make it work for us?

We can give to the causes that are important to us.

We can invest in the people and ideas that we trust and believe in.

We can choose to spend on things and in places that reflect our values.

We can choose to not spend on things and in places that don't.

We can resist buying more than we need—for the sake of the environment and as a rejection of the religion of capitalism.

We can responsibly use our resources in ways that will make the future better for more than just ourselves.

We should never be too ashamed to find out what we don't know. Learn about where your taxes are going and how those who represent you are stewarding your money. Learn about new models of cooperative economics that communities have used to take care of themselves and live in harmony with the world. And above all, remember your worth and your power as living, breathing people in a free world. No matter where you fall in the 99 percent, you are someone of value and your money can be a tool to shape the world you want to see. Maybe, if we use our dollars just right, one day it'll all make sense.

UNREASONABLE LOVING

The power to heal, save, and fix the world—and our nation and our communities within it—is the act of loving. Loving interrupts our self-centered longing for change and forces us to actually be the lovers. bell hooks calls it "living by an ethic of love."

To be loving every day politically is to resist and reject politics based on hatred, division, domination, and violence. Loving means to serve, to give, and to seek justice (Cornel West famously said that justice is what love looks like in public).

But even that might seem too easy if we don't do it right.

There have been many times when I felt as if loving was an insufficient reaction to what was going on in our world. I was more interested in power, in defeating political opponents. But that's because I was thinking of love as just "niceness," "kindness." That is not the loving that will change the world. To transform our environment, we can't just love in any ol' kind of way. The forces of division and hatred are too strong to love in a comfortable, easy way.

We have to give what my favorite writer, Kiese Laymon, calls "unreasonable loving."

We have to practice the kind of love that Dr. King described as "spontaneous, unmotivated and groundless." Or what a dear friend of mine, activist Valarie Kaur, calls "revolutionary love."

Whichever adjective you prefer, the meaning is the same: We have to love in hard, illogical, radical, that-don't-make-no-sense ways. Loving in this way doesn't discriminate against who is worthy and who isn't. Loving like this involves sacrifices and sometimes puts others' interests ahead of our own. This loving protects those who are in need of protecting, even if we don't understand them, and it comforts those who are afraid. This loving defaults to believing victims and listens, even when we think we know the answer.

The kind of loving we need is extreme. But it's not hard to imagine what would happen if we all committed to it. This may not be a complicated solution to what is broken in our world, but it also isn't an easy one. The kind of loving that we must do is hard—it requires effort and a commitment that pushes us past our comfort zones. But beyond-comfort-zone loving always transforms the lover just as much as it transforms the loved. There has never been a time when I made a political, active choice to love and regretted it. Each time I have walked away somehow . . . bigger. Stronger. Softer. More whole. And with more hope that things can change.

What if we decided that we would vote, give, and act in a way that prioritizes loving over self-interest? That places a love ethic over our assumptions and judgments?

Would we be able to show mercy to violent offenders? Offer opportunities to F students? Give people second chances? Open our own homes to children in need or as sanctuary for immigrants? Would we be more sensitive and let our own hearts break just a little bit more?

So let's each day ask ourselves how can we be *more* loving in our work to change the world. The answers will surprise you.

THE TIME FOR DOUBT

Personally, I can't imagine trying to fix the broken systems of this world without first speaking to the broken hearts and feeding the soul. And if it were up to me, no one would ever try to achieve social transformation without spiritual transformation. Faith offers us a ready-made framework for ideas like renewal, forgiveness, stewardship, responsibility, healing, and a belief in something bigger than ourselves when we ourselves have failed. Why not use it?

But . . . that's just my opinion. And I know that many people don't share it. For a lot people, many of whom I admire and respect, there is a strict separation of the spiritual and the political. But guess what?

Even in spaces where there is no talk of religion, faith, or spirituality, belief is all around. We may think because we don't talk about God or Spirit that we don't have a faith, but America is actually full of believers. Believers in democracy. Believers in elections. Believers in capitalism. Believers in politicians and celebrities. Believers in data and polls. Believers in facts. Or as my friend Casey Gerald put it in his masterful TED Talk, *The Gospel of Doubt*, "We pray to the gods of our time, the prophecy of Brené Brown or Tony Robbins, the Bible of the *New Yorker* or the *Harvard Business Review*, the church of TED."

For years we put our trust in these things and assumed that they had the answers to all that is wrong with the world. We had . . . *certainty*. And then, just like in the crooked room story of belief and faith, everything changed. What happens when the things you believe fail you in epic ways? The markets we put our faith in crashed. None of the polls and data that we trusted so deeply predicted Hillary Clinton's loss. Facts no longer function as evidence of truth. What happens when everything seems to be uncertain?

You embrace the new story with wonder and curiosity. And you live in the questions. It's time for us to collectively ask questions about who we are and whether or not the systems and structures that make up the foundation of our communities actually work.

Small questions yield small answers. Big questions yield big answers. And we are in a moment that calls for big, hard questions. We just can't tiptoe around them anymore. Start from a premise of curiosity and ask questions about the foundations of what you've always believed. What if we had no prisons? What if we all had access to fresh, healthy food? Ask questions about capitalism or representative democracy. Don't just question our leaders. Question our entire idea and model of leadership. And what about the American Dream? Go ahead and question that too.

When I say this to people, their first response often is "And then what? Just . . . ask questions? How is that a strategy?" I say, "It's the beginning of one." Embracing wonder and curiosity means being okay with questions that don't have immediate, easy, or complete answers. But it's the only way that we make space for the answers to arise.

When we start with the certainty that our two-party system is good, all we can do is try to elect more people into the same roles in the same institutions with the same low rate of voter engagement. But when we question that premise entirely, we can begin being honest about how both parties have failed us, and what system might really reflect our nuanced and fluid political goals.

When we start with the belief that society's "best and brightest" are the most educated, we end up with a leadership caste that is Ivy League–educated, white, and male. But when we begin to question what we think of as the requirements for good leadership, or even the idea of having a single charismatic leader altogether, we suddenly see the genius and brilliance in the parts of our country where we never looked before.

When we start from the premise that prisons are necessary, all we think about is being "tougher on crime." But if we question that premise entirely, we may learn about more compassionate and effective responses that actually *reduce* crime in a way that incarceration does not.

When we start from certainty that America is inherently "better" than every other place in the world, we only look within our borders for solutions to our problems. But when we question, we open ourselves up to being a more humble and teachable partner on the world stage.

Need I go on?

Remember: Asking the question does not imply an outright rejection of the status quo. Challenging the certainty of my religion actually helped me to ultimately embrace even more the simplicity of my faith and many of the traditions that I loved. Similarly, questioning America's superiority doesn't mean that you don't love your country, and questioning how we vote doesn't mean that you want to live under an oligarchy. It means that you no longer have certainty that the way things have always been done is the way to go into the future. It's actually a rather hopeful approach, if you think about it: Asking hard questions means that ultimately you have so much faith in humanity that no question is too outlandish, no idea too radical, to somehow, some way, save it.

EPILOGUE

In the years since I first stepped away from my life and the old stories, I have learned so very much. Starting from the simple conviction that we all deserve better than this—a stagnant, suffocating, unfulfilling way of life—led me to a life that is better, more vibrant, and more powerful than I ever thought possible.

Today, as I write this, I live in Los Angeles, write, speak, teach, host shows and events, make content, and have built a creative program at one of the biggest social media platforms in the world (Snapchat). By the time you read this, who knows how many of those pieces may have changed. My life, like a story, is unfolding every day, with new plot points, new characters, new settings, and new chapters. And I am, as we talked about in the beginning of this book, constantly wayfinding, responding to new information and new realities, and experimenting to fulfill the purpose for my life. But what remains the same is that as I pursue that purpose—using my voice to help others transform themselves and the world around them—I see very clearly how stories can and will forever be my most powerful tool, just as they are yours.

Remember: There is nothing—no fear, no job, no circumstance, no bank account, no relationship, no opinion—that will have more impact on the choices that we make and the life that we are working to build than the stories that we choose to reject, accept, and believe.

Thank you so much for examining and rewriting yours alongside me. I can't wait to see what your true story looks like. The world is waiting.

ACKNOWLEDGMENTS

To Daddy. I feel your spirit every single day. You left *such* big shoes to fill, but I'm not a little girl anymore (and my shoes certainly aren't small) so I finally feel up to the task of trying. I love you forever.

Mommy, there's no me without you. Literally. Thank you for loving me so well and for being so supportive that you made all of your friends pre-order this book. I hope I make you proud.

To Ayinde, my greatest listener, my hype man, my comic relief, my chicken nugget supplier, my love for a lifetime: There isn't enough space here to say all the ways you've cared for and helped me during the writing of this book, so I'll just say this: rubber bottom, rocket ship, gems.

Allyson, the best sister, duet partner, friend, and human I've ever met. I basically wrote this whole thing for you, so can this be your birthday gift this year? Thanks for reading my drafts, accepting me as I am, and being my greatest inspiration.

To my entire family, especially: Aunt Gigi, Uncle Ronald, Syd, Uncle Ronnie, Aunt Kim, Erik, David, Curtis, Moriah, Uncle Michael,

Luke, Uncle Elder, Godmommy Gail, and all of my extended family, blood and chosen. Thank you for being my favorite people.

To the friends who cheered me on at various stages of this process and always had the right word to say at the right time, especially on days when I wanted to give up: Kali Simon, Franchesca Ramsey, Casey Gerald, dream hampton, Sean Carasso, Najeeba Syeed, Latham Thomas, Xana O'Neill, and everyone I forgot to mention.

To my Cornerstone family, thank you for praying for me, for encouraging me to always pursue my dreams, and for being my forever village. John 10:10 forever.

To my agent, Laura Yorke, for convincing me that what I wanted to say really was worth finally turning into a book, and to Pam Liflander, for spending hours asking me questions, challenging my arguments, and helping me organize my thoughts, ideas, and words.

To all the dark-skinned girls. You're my motivation. I see you. I got us.

And to every single person who has ever written me a note, emailed me, tweeted me, listened to my podcast, watched one of my shows or videos, given me an opportunity, or done anything at all to let me know you believe in, support, and trust me, thank you. There are so many things that I am not, but so much of what I am is because you let me know that I matter. I hope everyone has someone to gift them that same knowing.

And if you don't, hear it now from me: Thank you for being you.